Mary Berry has published over sixty cookery books, regularly contributes to magazines, television and radio shows, and ran the AGA workshops cookery school for sixteen years. Mary was trained at the Bath College of Home Economics, has teaching and catering qualifications and Paris Cordon Bleu.

Happily married with two grown-up children, Mary lives in Buckinghamshire.

Mary Berry

Fast Cakes

sphere

SPHERE

First published in Great Britain in 1981 by Piatkus Books
Published by Sphere Books Ltd 1983
Published by Warner Books 1993
Published by Time Warner Paperbacks 2002
Published by Time Warner Books 2005
This paperback edition published in 2009 by Sphere
Reprinted 2009, 2011 (three times), 2012 (twice)

ISBN 978-0-7515-0490-3

Typeset in American Garamond by M Rules
Printed and bound in Great Britain by
Clays Ltd, St Ives plc

Papers used by Sphere are from well-managed forests
and other responsible sources.

MIX
Paper from
responsible sources
FSC® C104740

Sphere
An imprint of
Little, Brown Book Group
100 Victoria Embankment
London EC4Y 0DY

An Hachette UK Company
www.hachette.co.uk

www.littlebrown.co.uk

Contents

Fast Cakes

Introduction

I have friends who make cakes because they love baking; and other friends who make them only under duress, usually because they have promised in a moment of madness to provide something for a local fête or school bazaar and a cake-offering was all they could think of on the spur of the moment.

I know – because I have been asked – why many people are put off the idea of making cakes. 'It's such a business!' they tell me. 'All that creaming of butter and sugar. I never seem to have the butter soft enough. And then the tins have to be lined and everything has to be just so. It's all right for *you*,' they add accusingly, 'you enjoy it!'

Well, so I do. But they are quite wrong if they think that you have to take a whole day off in order to make cakes successfully. Cakes teabreads and biscuits, too can be made quickly and easily with the minimum of fuss and trouble. There is no need to bother with fancy tins or piping bags to produce an informal yet professional finish to all kinds of teatime delicacies. When I sat down to list the different varieties which could conceivably be used in a book on rapid cake-making, I was amazed how quickly I covered the paper. In quite a short time I had written down well over one hundred and fifty recipe suggestions, all of which are given in detail further on in this book. Among them must be several dozen to tempt even the most reluctant cake-maker!

Basic equipment
Baking tins. All the recipes use one or other of the following tins:
✓ 2 × 7 inch (17.5 cm) round sandwich tins
✓ 1 × 7 inch (17.5 cm) deep cake tin
✓ 1 × 8 inch (20 cm) deep cake tin – round or square
These four are best with loose bases because they are easier to turn out and there is no need to line them.

1

✓ 1 × 2 lb (900 g) loaf tin
✓ 1 × 1 lb (450 g) loaf tin
✓ 1 × 11 × 7 inch (27.5 × 17.5 cm) rectangular tin
✓ 1 × 12 × 9 inch (30 × 22.5 cm) rectangular roasting tin
✓ 2 × bun tins
✓ 2 large, heavy, flat baking trays

When the cakes are cooked, they have to be cooled. It helps, therefore, to have:
2 large cooling racks – but you can, of course, always use the grid from your grill pan.

Preparation equipment. I find that I use:
✓ A selection of ovenglass bowls in which to mix the ingredients.
✓ 1 plastic or rubber scraper. This cuts out waste, enabling you to get all the mixture off the sides of the bowls. It makes the children cross, however, because there is not enough mixture left in the bowl for them to lick!
✓ 1 palette knife for spreading icing.
✓ 1 long fish slice for lifting out slices of cake from roasting tins.
✓ A selection of measuring spoons for measuring such ingredients as baking powder or spices – all amounts given in the recipes are for level spoonfuls.
✓ 1 small or medium oval wire whisk for beating eggs or small amounts of cream. It gives a light mixture and, if you do not have one already, it can be bought quite cheaply from any hardware shop.
✓ 1 wooden spatula or spoon. I prefer using a spatula because it is flat on both sides and is easy to scrape clean.
✓ Greaseproof paper for lining cake tins which do not have loose bases. Time-saving tip: use a spare moment to cut several circles to fit the tin you most often use and store them in a bag in a drawer.

✓ Silicone paper – sometimes called vegetable non-stick parchment – made by Bakewell, it is available in packets or on a roll from most good stationers. It is invaluable for lining the baking sheet when you make meringues or other sugary things as it really is non-stick. Best of all, the same paper can be used time and time again. I just shake off the sugar, fold the paper and put it back in the packet for next time. You can draw circles on it to use as a guide when shaping meringue rings or pavlova.

✓ Foil for lining tins when strength is needed, and useful afterwards for placing between layers of cakes in storage tins.

✓ Food mixer. Whether you have a table model or a hand-held mixer, follow the instructions given in your mixer book.

✓ Food processor. I have tested several and, again, it is important to follow the instructions which come with the machine.

Useful storage aids and equipment

✓ Cling film is excellent for wrapping cakes because it keeps the moisture in. Its great advantage is that you can see what it contains!

✓ Kitchen roll. How did we ever exist without it? At one time, cloths and tea towels had to be used for covering and wrapping foods and these involved constant washing and drying so that they could be used again. Paper is useful for placing between layers of shortbreads, etc, in storage tins. It is absorbent and handy for wiping up spills.

✓ Airtight storage tins. Remember to store cakes and biscuits separately. If you put them together, the biscuits will go soft.

✓ Freezer. Strictly speaking, not essential, but a tremendous boon to modern living. All cakes freeze extremely well, except for those containing breakfast cereal. Iced cakes are best frozen uncovered until they are firm, then wrapped carefully and returned to the freezer to freeze solid. I try not to keep cakes in the freezer longer than three months, as those which have been kept for longer seem to lose a little of their flavour when they are thawed out. Fruit cakes and shortbreads, however, can stay in the freezer for many months, and, indeed, keep well in an airtight tin in a cool, dry storage cupboard. You may well ask why bother to freeze them at all? Well, frankly, most kitchens are too warm for ideal storage conditions and some have insufficient room. The freezer not only maintains the cakes in good condition but it is also a deterrent to thieving fingers! The family is unlikely to raid the freezer and eat frozen shortbread, for example, but a tin is an open invitation! Incidentally, there is no need to freeze meringues, but you can if you wish.

Preparation methods

All-in-one means exactly what it says. Everything goes into the same container at once – either into a bowl for mixing with an electric food mixer, or into a large saucepan for mixing by melting (used, for example, in making gingerbread). Apart from the speed of preparation, this also cuts down on the washing up.

I prefer to use a high fat spread over 59% for baking instead of butter. Spread for baking simplifies the process because you do not have to remove it from the refrigerator and give it time to soften before you use it.

Do use self-raising flour *and* baking powder for the all-in-one method. Because mixing in this way is so quick, far quicker than in traditional cake-making, there is not enough air beaten into the mixture to make it rise, and using baking powder as well as self-raising flour gives the extra lift necessary. But *do stick to the amount of baking powder given in the recipe.* If you use too much, the cake will rise quickly when it first goes into the oven and then flop down before it is properly cooked.

Using a food mixer. A mixer is perfect for all-in-one mixtures – my own is in constant use – but do take care not to over mix. Check through your instruction book for any special tips.

I often put more mixture than I really should into my Kenwood Chef. I prevent the flour from showering all over the floor by carefully covering the front end of the machine and the bowl with a teacloth. If you do the same, remember to stand by the machine while it is mixing in order to see that the teacloth does not accidentally slip into the mixture and get caught up in the spindle.

Tips for success every time
Please read before trying any of the recipes!

1. Choose a recipe that is going to be popular with the family. Of all the recipes I give, some, I must admit, are more popular with my family than others. If it is any help to you, these are the ones we enjoy most and which have become my stand-bys:

   For everyday
   Just Rock Cakes
   Mincemeat Cake
   Marmalade Cake
   Almond Bakewell Tart
   Fruit Malt Loaf
   Special Scones
   Banana, Date and Cherry Loaf
   Ginger Fairings
   Botermoppen
   Easy Apple Cake
   Lemon Cake

For special occasions
Coffee Fudge Bars
Superb Carrot Cake
Pineapple and Raisin Cake
Coffee and Praline Meringue
Raspberry Cream Pavlova
Special Apricot Cake
Grapefruit or Orange Cheesecake
Brandy Snaps
Chocolate Juliette
Grantham Gingerbreads
Strawberry Shortbread
Victoriana Christmas Cake
Chocolate Eclairs

With children in mind
Chocolate Caramel Shortbread
Caramel Crunch Bars
Caroline's Chocolate Slab
Flap Jacks (older children)
First-Rate Chocolate Cake
Chocolate Cream Fingers

2. Read the recipe through carefully, checking that you have all the ingredients in the larder or store cupboard and also that you have time to make it and bake it. If you have to nip out and collect the children from school or see a neighbour, select a recipe that uses the all-in-a-bowl method. The mixture can be prepared and put in the tins ready for baking when you return. The uncooked mixture will not spoil if, as so often happens with me, the ten minutes you thought you would be away turns into half an hour. Cakes already in the oven are not so accommodating!

3. Before switching on the oven or, in the case of a gas oven, lighting it, put the oven shelves in their correct position. One cake is usually baked with the shelf in the centre position. With two cakes one is usually placed above centre, the other below. But check the instructions given in the recipe book that comes with your cooker. With an electric fan oven, for example, there is even baking on all shelves. With solid fuel cookers, the temperature cannot be adjusted and it is even more important to follow the manufacturers' instructions or your own experience.

4. On gas and electric cookers, set the oven temperature sufficiently early for the right temperature to be reached by the time the cake is ready to be baked.

5. Weigh ingredients. In many recipes, time can be saved by weighing them straight into the mixing bowl. Follow the order given in the list of ingredients, ticking them off, if you like, so that no ingredient is accidentally forgotten. Incidentally, I have deliberately left salt out of most of the recipes. I find it makes no difference to the flavour and using it means one more thing to remember!

6. Prepare tins. Here is a confession: if I am in a great hurry, I do not bother to grease biscuit-baking trays. When the biscuits or maybe rock cakes are cooked, I carefully ease them off the tray with a palette knife or fish slice. With experience, you will soon find out when you can or cannot do this.

7. Follow the method conscientiously. I do not believe that you can think of a short cut which I have not already tried! The method I give for each recipe is one which, from experience, I find works best. So if you are the sort of person who likes to experiment, may I respectfully suggest that you wait until you have had a go at doing it my way first!

8. The temperature of the oven is most important when baking. If you are not absolutely certain that your oven temperature

is correct, beg, borrow or buy an oven thermometer and carry out a check yourself. Buying a thermometer is cheaper than asking a utility engineer to visit your home and test your thermostat. Alternatively, if in practice you notice that your cakes always take a longer or shorter time to cook than is given in the recipe, adjust the oven setting accordingly next time and *make a note of it*.

9. Never open the oven door during the early part of the baking time or move the cake tin in the oven. Both actions will make the cake sink in the middle.

10. Remember that, with most ovens, if you batch-bake several trays of buns or cakes at a time, they will take longer to cook than a solitary cake. Keep an eye on them during the latter part of the baking and, lifting them carefully without banging, move the tins or trays around so that each batch is evenly browned. Forgetful cooks would be well advised to use a pinger-timer to remind them to check. The timer, of course, should be set to go off at a shorter interval than the baking time in the recipe.

How much mixture a cake tin takes

✓ 2 × 7 inch (17.5 cm) sandwich tins take 1 lb (450 g) at 180°c/160Fan/Gas 4 and need 25 to 30 minutes cooking time.

✓ 2 × 8 inch (20 cm) sandwich tins take 1½ lb (675 g) at 180°c/160Fan/Gas 4 and need 35 minutes cooking time.

✓ 18 small queen cakes take 1 lb (450 g) at 200°c/180Fan/Gas 6 and need 15 minutes cooking time.

✓ 1 × 7 inch (17.5 cm) round cake tin takes 2½ lb (1.1 kg) at 160°c/140Fan/Gas 3 for about 1½ hours for a fruit cake.

✓ 1 × 8 inch (20 cm) round cake tin takes 3¾ lb (1.7 kg) at 160°c/140Fan/Gas 3 and needs about 2½ hours for a fruit cake.

✓ 1 × 7 inch (17.5 cm) square tin as for an 8 inch (20 cm) round tin.

Whisked cakes
✓ 2 × 7 inch (17.5 cm) sandwich tins take a 3 egg mix.
✓ 2 × 8 inch (20 cm) sandwich tins take a 4 egg mix.
  Bake at 190°c/170Fan/Gas 5 for 20 minutes for the small size and 25 minutes for the large size.
✓ 1 × Swiss roll tin 13 × 9 inches (32.5 × 22.5 cm) takes a 3 egg mix; bake at 220°c/200Fan/Gas 7 for 10 minutes.

How to know when a cake is done

There is no great mystery in cooking a cake. It is done when it looks and smells ready. In most cases, the principal signs are when the cake shrinks slightly from the sides of the tin and when the top of the cake springs back after being pressed lightly with the finger.

Large fruit cakes, however, do need a further test. Simply push a fine metal skewer into the centre of the cake and if it comes out clean and shiny, the cake is ready. If the skewer has some of the cake mixture clinging to it, close the oven door and cook for a few minutes longer, checking again from time to time. Sometimes, the cake is not quite done in the middle but the top is getting brown and the currants on the surface seem to be burning. In this case, place a piece of foil lightly on the top, lower the oven temperature and leave to cook for longer.

With biscuits and shortbread, test by eye, checking that the colour is right, not only on the top but on the underneath as well. Outside ones may do slightly more quickly than those in the middle. In this case remove them to a wire rack to cool and return the rest to the oven for a few minutes extra cooking time.

Cooling

Leave cakes in the tin to cool for a while before turning them out onto a wire rack (see under individual recipes). To turn the cake out quickly and simply without breaking it, run a knife round the edge of the tin before inverting the tin. If the tin has been lined, turn upside down onto a folded tea towel, take away the tin, peel off the paper and transfer the cake to the cooling rack.

With Victoria sandwiches, I turn out the sponges onto the rack and then *replace the tins over them*. This prevents the moisture from evaporating while the cakes are cooling and it does not make the sponges soggy.

Help! It has all gone wrong

Frankly, I do not think anything should go wrong with your baking efforts but just in case you do have the occasional failure, here is a guide to the possible reasons:

All-in-one mixtures

Coarse texture	Too much baking powder
Collar edge on cake	Rising of cake was too rapid and it then sank. One of two causes: either the cake was placed on too high a shelf in the oven or there was too much baking powder in the mixture.
Damp, close texture	Cake was removed from the oven too soon
Domed, cracked top	Oven too hot or cake placed too high in oven
Hollow top	Mixture beaten too long; too slow an oven; cooking time too short; spread for baking allowed to become oily during very hot weather

Pale in colour although fully cooked	Oven too cool or cake placed on too low a shelf

Melted mixtures

Cracked top	Too much baking powder, syrup or treacle; too hot an oven, door opened too early
Doughy texture	Too much flour or baking powder, not enough liquid
Hard on outside	Too much liquid or syrup; oven too hot

Whisked mixtures

Specks of uncooked flour	Poor whisking; flour not mixed in properly
Sticky, damp texture when cold, sticking to sides of tin	Usually caused by being in too much of a hurry and skimping each stage; thus ingredients not correctly measured; under-whisking so that the sugar has not properly dissolved; under-baking; tin badly prepared. Any or all of these will give sticky results.
Too shallow, not risen	Insufficient whisking; too cool an oven; not enough baking powder
Uneven rising	Flour not folded in properly; oven shelves not level; mixture unevenly distributed in the tin before baking
Wrinkled top to cake	Under-baking; tin too small

Tray Bakes

I deal for family tea and children's parties because making them requires so little trouble that it leaves you free to concentrate on other party specialities. The joy of tray bakes is that they are made, cooled and iced in one tin – a roasting tin is perfect – so that you do not have to bother with cooling racks; and they take up little space in a busy kitchen. Icing is simply poured over the cooked and cooled cake, smoothed with a palette knife and left to set; no spills, no mess. The cake can then be cut to whatever size pieces you prefer. Small, two-bite-size pieces are best for children's parties as there is less possibility of any wasted cake.

Tray Bakes

The basic recipe is economical and made with large families, coffee mornings and bazaars in mind. Ideally, ice the cakes in the tin and, when set, lift out with a palette knife.

Making time 10 minutes
Baking time about 35 to 40 minutes

6 oz (175 g) spread for baking
8 oz (225 g) self-raising flour
1½ level teaspoons baking powder
6 oz (175 g) caster sugar
3 eggs
3 tablespoons milk

Heat the oven to 180°c/160Fan/Gas 4 and then grease and line with greased greaseproof paper a meat roasting tin about 12 × 9 inches (30 × 22.5 cm).

Put the spread, flour, baking powder, sugar, eggs and milk together in a large roomy bowl and beat well for about 2 minutes until well blended. Turn the mixture into the tin and smooth the top. Bake in the oven for about 35 to 40 minutes until the cake has shrunk from the sides of the tin and springs back when pressed in the centre with your fingertips.

Leave to cool in the tin and then ice as required. Cut into 21 pieces.

Makes 21 pieces

Variations

Fruit Cake

Add 6 to 8 oz (175 to 225 g) currants to the other ingredients in the bowl and then sprinkle 1 level tablespoon demerara sugar over the cake halfway through the cooking time.

Lemon Cake

Add the grated rind of 1½ lemons to the cake ingredients. When the cake comes out of the oven, mix the juice of 1½ lemons with 6 oz (175g) caster or granulated sugar and spoon over the hot cake. If the lemons have a lot of juice, the lemon and sugar mixture will be runny, otherwise it will be more like a sugary paste which has to be spread over the cake with the back of a spoon.

Chocolate Cake

First, in the mixing bowl, blend 3 level tablespoons cocoa with 3 tablespoons of hot water and then cool slightly. Add the remaining ingredients and make the cake as usual but omit the milk unless the cake mixture seems very stiff. Even so, it should only be necessary to add about 1 tablespoonful. Leave to cool in the tin.

Chocolate Icing

Melt 3 oz (75 g) butter or spread for baking in a small saucepan and then stir in 2 oz (50 g) sieved cocoa and cook over a gentle heat for 1 minute. Remove from the heat and then stir in 8 oz (225 g) sieved icing sugar and 2 tablespoons milk. Beat well until the icing has thickened and then spread over the cake. Leave to set.

Bakewell Open Tart

Line the tin with shortcrust pastry made with 6 oz (175 g) flour and 3 oz (75 g) spread for baking. Spread the pastry with raspberry jam. Top with the basic cake mixture made up using 2 eggs and 4 oz (100 g) spread for baking i.e. cutting all ingredients by one third – and add to this ½ teaspoon almond essence. If liked, sprinkle the sponge mixture with flaked almonds.

Black Treacle Cake

Use only 4½ oz (112 g) caster sugar in the basic mixture, then add 7 oz (200 g) black treacle and 1½ level teaspoons mixed spice. When the cake is cooked and cold it looks nice if sprinkled with sieved icing sugar.

Cherry Tray Bake

Make and bake a basic tray bake sponge. When cool, ice with a vanilla icing made with 3 oz (75 g) spread for baking, 8 oz (225 g) sieved icing sugar, 1 tablespoon milk and vanilla essence to flavour. Spread over the top of the cake, mark into bars and decorate each bar with halved glacé cherries.

Moist Chocolate and Orange Squares

This tray bake is ideal to make for a coffee morning because, with the ground almonds and golden syrup, it keeps well and may be made in advance. Store in an airtight tin.

Making time about 5 minutes
Baking time about 1¼ hours

6 oz (175 g) spread for baking
6 oz (175 g) caster sugar
6 oz (175 g) golden syrup
2 large eggs
2 oz (50 g) ground almonds
1 oz (25 g) cocoa, sieved
7 oz (200 g) plain flour
½ level teaspoon bicarbonate of soda dissolved in ¼ pint (150 ml) milk
grated rind of 1 large orange

Orange butter cream
3 oz (75 g) spread for baking
8 oz (225 g) icing sugar, sieved
3 tablespoons orange juice

Heat the oven to 150°c/130Fan/Gas 2 and then grease and line with greased greaseproof paper a meat tin 12 × 9 inches (30 × 22.5 cm).

Put all the ingredients together in a large roomy bowl and beat well for about 2 minutes until the mixture is well blended. Turn into the tin, smooth the top and then bake in the oven for about 1¼ to 1½ hours until the cake has shrunk from the sides of the tin and springs back when pressed with your finger. Leave to cool in the tin and then turn out and remove the paper.

For the orange butter cream: put all the ingredients together in a bowl and beat well until they are smooth and blended – this will take 2 to 3 minutes. Spread the cream over the top of the cake, mark attractively with a knife or fork and leave to set. When ready, cut into 20 squares.

Makes 20 chocolate and orange squares

Coffee Fudge Bars

These bars have a very mild coffee flavour which, strangely enough, is popular with children. You can leave out the nuts but the result will not be as good.

Making time about 10 minutes
Baking time about 40 minutes

6 oz (175 g) spread for baking
6 oz (175 g) caster sugar
3 large eggs
2 oz (50 g) chopped walnuts
1 tablespoon coffee essence
6 oz (175 g) self-raising flour
1½ level teaspoons baking powder

Coffee fudge icing
3 oz (75 g) spread for baking
8 oz (225 g) icing sugar, sieved
1 tablespoon milk
1 tablespoon coffee essence
2 oz (50 g) chopped walnuts

Heat the oven to 160°c/140Fan/Gas 3 and grease and line with greased greaseproof paper a large tin 12 × 9 inches (30 × 22.5 cm).

Measure the spread, sugar, eggs, walnuts and coffee essence into a bowl and then sieve in the flour and baking powder. Beat well until smooth and blended.

Turn into the prepared tin and smooth the top. Then cook for 40 minutes or until the cake is well risen and shrinking away from the sides of the tin. The cake will spring back when lightly pressed with the fingertips. Leave to cool in the tin.

For the icing: put the spread, icing sugar, milk and coffee essence in a bowl and beat until smooth. Spread over the cake and then sprinkle with walnuts. Cut into 20 bars.

Makes 20 coffee fudge bars

Pale Ginger Squares

If you have had a jar of stem ginger on the shelf for a while this is a good way of putting it to use. The squares are topped with a simple ginger icing.

Making time about 10 minutes
Baking time about 35 to 40 minutes

6 oz (175 g) spread for baking
6 oz (175 g) light brown sugar
6 oz (175 g) self-raising flour
1½ level teaspoons baking powder
1½ level teaspoons ground ginger
3 eggs
2 tablespoons milk

Topping
1½ oz (40 g) very finely chopped stem ginger
6 oz (175 g) icing sugar, sieved
2 to 3 tablespoons ginger syrup

Heat the oven to 180°c/160Fan/Gas 4 and then grease and line with greased greaseproof paper a meat tin 12 × 9 inches (30 × 22.5 cm).

Put the spread, sugar, flour, baking powder, ginger, eggs and milk in a large bowl and beat well for 2 minutes until well blended. Turn into the tin, smooth the top and bake in the oven for about 20 minutes. Then sprinkle over the finely chopped ginger and continue cooking for a further 15 minutes or until the sponge is golden brown and springs back when pressed in the centre with your fingertips.

Leave to cool in the tin and then turn out, remove the paper and put on a wire rack.

Blend the icing sugar with the ginger syrup until smooth and then spoon over the cake and leave to set. Cut into 21 squares.

Makes 21 pale ginger squares

Variation

Dark Ginger and Walnut Squares

Use dark soft brown sugar and 1 tablespoon black treacle in place of 1 tablespoon of milk. Stir in 2 oz (50 g) chopped walnuts instead of the ginger. Do not ice, but sprinkle with sieved icing sugar.

Sponge Fruit Slice

Making a sponge mixture with condensed milk gives it a lovely flavour and texture. Ring the changes by using whichever fruit you have in the store cupboard – if liked, add a few chopped nuts.

Making time about 15 minutes
Baking time 30 to 35 minutes

8 oz (227 g) packet shortcrust pastry
about 2 rounded tablespoons jam
4 oz (100 g) spread for baking
6 oz (175 g) can condensed milk
½ teaspoon vanilla essence
2 large eggs
4 oz (100 g) self-raising flour
6 oz (175 g) sultanas

Heat the oven to 190°c/170Fan/Gas 5.

Roll out the pastry and line the base and sides of a tin 11 × 7 × 1 inch (27.5 × 17.5 × 2.5 cm). Crimp the edges and spread the base with jam.

Place all the other ingredients in a bowl and beat thoroughly until they are blended. Spoon into the pastry case and smooth the top. Then bake in the oven for 30 to 35 minutes until the sponge is well risen and golden brown.

Remove from the oven and leave to cool in the tin.

When quite cold cut into 16 slices.

Makes 16 sponge fruit slices

Small Cakes

These cakes are marvellous stand-bys to have in the freezer because you can control the rate at which they disappear by only putting out a limited number at any one time. With a large cake, once it has been cut it might as well be finished. Small cakes are also one of the quickest forms of baking. Apart from the fact that they require less cooking time, preparation is also speeded up because you can use paper cases instead of going through all the business of greasing or lining tins.

Queen Cakes

From this basic mixture a variety of other small cakes may be made. If you use paper cases, stand them in a 12-holed bun tin as it helps to keep them in a good shape and prevents them toppling over. If you intend icing the cakes in their paper cases make sure that you do not fill the cases too full.

Making time about 10 minutes
Baking time about 15 minutes

4 oz (100 g) spread for baking
4 oz (100 g) caster sugar
4 oz (100 g) self-raising flour
2 eggs
1 level teaspoon baking powder

Heat the oven to 200°c/180Fan/Gas 6 and have ready about 18 paper cases set in bun tins. The number of cases required will vary slightly if the cakes are to be iced or extra ingredients added.

Place all the ingredients together in a bowl and beat well for 2 to 3 minutes until they are well blended and smooth.

Divide between the paper cases and bake in the oven for about 15 minutes until the cakes are well risen and golden brown. Lift out and cool on a wire rack.

Makes about 18 cakes

Variations

Butterfly Cakes

Cut a slice from the top of each cake and cut this slice in half. Pipe a swirl of butter icing in the centre and then replace the two half slices of cake into the icing, butterfly fashion.

Chocolate Cakes

Replace ½ to 1 oz (12 to 25 g) flour with the same amount of cocoa.

Coffee Cakes

Dissolve 1 level teaspoon instant coffee powder in the beaten eggs before adding to the bowl.

Iced Queen Cakes

If there is a little of the rim of the paper case above the level of the cakes then it is easy to ice the top. Make up 2 to 3 oz (50 to 75 g) icing sugar with a little water and flavouring. Pour it over the top of the cakes and decorate as liked.

Currant Cakes

Add 1 oz (25 g) currants to the basic queen cake recipe.

Orange or Lemon Cakes

Add the grated rind of a small lemon or orange to the basic queen cake recipe and then use the juice to make a little glacé icing to pour over the top of the cakes.

Basic White Meringues

Make meringues by this foolproof method and I guarantee success. Use non-stick silicone paper, which can be bought from any good stationer, and may be brushed off after use and used again and again.

Making time about 15 minutes
Baking time 3 to 4 hours

4 egg whites
8 oz (225 g) caster sugar
whipping cream

Heat the oven to 120°c/100Fan/Gas ¼ and line two baking sheets with silicone paper.

Place the egg whites in a large bowl and whisk on high speed with an electric or hand rotary whisk until they form soft peaks. Add the sugar, a teaspoonful at a time, whisking well after each addition, until all the sugar has been added. Using two dessertspoons, spoon the meringue out onto the baking sheets, putting 12 meringues on each tray.

Bake in the oven for 3 to 4 hours until the meringues are firm and dry and will lift easily from the silicone paper. They will be a very pale off-white or slightly darker if you have used soft brown sugar.

Whisk the cream until it is thick and use it to sandwich the meringues together.

Makes 12 double meringues

Variation

Brown Meringues

Make exactly as above but use 8 oz (225 g) light soft brown sugar instead of caster sugar.

Coconut Meringue Slices

These delicious fingers of sponge keep well. For a change, sprinkle the top with finely chopped glacé cherries.

Making time about 20 to 25 minutes
Baking time about 35 minutes

3 oz (75 g) spread for baking
4 oz (100 g) caster sugar
2 egg yolks
2 tablespoons milk
a few drops of vanilla essence
6 oz (175 g) self-raising flour

Topping
2 egg whites
2 oz (50 g) desiccated coconut
4 oz (100 g) caster sugar
flaked almonds

Heat the oven to 160°c/140Fan/Gas 3 and line with greased greaseproof paper a tin 11 × 7 × 1 inch deep (27.5 × 17.5 × 2.5 cm deep).

Cream the spread and sugar until soft and then beat in the egg yolks, milk and vanilla essence and lastly fold in the flour – the mixture will be quite stiff. Spread it carefully in a smooth layer over the base of the tin.

Whisk the egg whites with an electric or rotary hand whisk until stiff and then whisk in the coconut and caster sugar a teaspoon at a time. Spread over the cake and sprinkle the top with flaked almonds.

Bake in the oven for 35 minutes, by which time the meringue will be firm to the touch and a pale golden brown. Leave it to cool in the tin and when cold cut it into 16 slices.

Makes 16 slices

Chocolate Coconut Squares

These are very rich and fattening but quite delicious – you might find it is better to make double the quantity!

Making time about 15 minutes
Baking time about 30 minutes

3½ oz (100 g) bar plain chocolate
2 oz (50 g) spread for baking
4 oz (100 g) caster sugar
1 egg, beaten
4 oz (100 g) desiccated coconut
2 oz (50 g) glacé cherries, finely chopped

Line a 7 inch (17.5 cm) square tin with foil.

Break the chocolate into squares. Put them in a basin and stand it over a pan of hot water. Heat gently until the chocolate has melted, then pour it straight into the prepared tin and smooth so that the base is evenly covered. Put in the refrigerator and leave to set for about 10 minutes.

Meanwhile heat the oven to 180°c/160Fan/Gas 4. Cream the spread and sugar together until soft and then work in the egg, coconut and cherries and mix well. Spread over the set chocolate and then bake it in the oven for about 30 minutes until brown all over.

Remove from the oven and leave undisturbed until quite cold. Then turn out and peel away the foil. Cut into 12 squares or, if preferred, into fingers.

Makes 12 squares

Chocolate Éclairs

Everybody's favourite.

Making time about 15 minutes
Baking time about 20 minutes

2 oz (50 g) butter
¼ pint (150 ml) milk and water mixed
2½ oz (62 g) plain flour
2 eggs, beaten

Filling
½ pint (300 ml) whipping cream

Icing
8 oz (225 g) icing sugar
1 level tablespoon cocoa
1 tablespoon rum
1 to 2 tablespoons warm water

Heat the oven to 200°c/180Fan/Gas 6 and grease a baking sheet.

Put the butter and milk and water in a saucepan and bring to the boil, stirring occasionally. Remove from the heat and add the flour all at once and beat until the mixture forms a ball. Gradually beat in the eggs to make a smooth shiny paste.

Place the mixture in a piping bag fitted with a ½ inch (1.25 cm) plain pipe. Pipe 12 to 14 éclairs, each about 2 inches (5 cm) long onto the baking sheet. Bake in the oven for about 20 minutes until they are well risen and golden brown. Remove from the oven and split one side of each éclair so that the steam can escape. Leave to cool on a wire rack. Whisk the cream until it is thick and then use to fill each éclair

For the icing, sift the icing sugar and cocoa into a bowl and stir in the rum and just sufficient warm water to make a thick icing. Spear each éclair with a fork and dip the tops in the icing. Leave to set and then serve on the day that they are made and filled.

Makes 12 to 14 éclairs

Chocolate Oat Crunch

These are rather like a special flap jack with icing on the top and are always very popular.

Making time about 10 minutes
Baking time about 30 minutes

4 oz (100 g) spread for baking
2 oz (50 g) soft brown sugar
4 oz (100 g) self-raising flour
2 oz (50 g) quick porridge oats
2 level teaspoons cocoa

Icing
4 oz (100 g) icing sugar, sieved
2 level teaspoons cocoa, sieved
5 teaspoons warm water

Heat the oven to 160°c/140Fan/Gas 3 and grease a shallow 11 × 7 inch (27.5 × 17.5 cm) tin.

Cream the spread and sugar together until soft and then work in the flour, oats and cocoa and mix very thoroughly. Press into the tin and bake for about 30 minutes.

Blend the icing ingredients together and then pour it over the mixture while the latter is still warm. Leave to set and then cut into 18 fingers.

Makes 18 chocolate oat crunchies

Chocolate Brownies

These are rather rich but are always popular. They are ideal to bake for a coffee morning or a bring-and-buy sale.

Making time about 15 minutes
Baking time about 25 to 30 minutes

3½ oz (100 g) bar plain chocolate
4 oz (100 g) spread for baking
4 oz (100 g) caster sugar
1 egg, beaten
½ teaspoon vanilla essence
5 oz (150 g) plain flour
½ level teaspoon baking powder
2 oz (50 g) walnuts, roughly chopped
1 tablespoon milk

Heat the oven to 180°c/160Fan/Gas 4. Grease and line with greased greaseproof paper a 7 × 11 inch (17.5 × 27.5 cm) tin.

Break the chocolate into pieces, place them in a bowl and stand it over a pan of warm water on a gentle heat, stirring occasionally, until the chocolate has melted. Cool slightly.

Put the remaining ingredients in a bowl and beat them together for a minute. Then beat in the chocolate and continue beating for a further minute or two until they have reached a soft dropping consistency.

Turn the mixture into the tin and bake in the oven for 25 to 35 minutes or until the cake has shrunk from the sides of the tin and springs back when lightly touched with the fingertips.

Leave to cool in the tin for 15 minutes and then mark into 18 pieces. Leave it in the tin until quite cold, turn out and store in an airtight container.

Makes 18 brownies

Mincemeat Brownies

The addition of mincemeat to brownies gives a lovely flavour.

Making time 10 minutes
Baking time about 40 minutes

6 oz (175 g) self-raising flour
2 oz (50 g) spread for baking
6 oz (175 g) dark soft brown sugar
1 egg
4 tablespoons mincemeat

Heat the oven to 180°c/160Fan/Gas 4. Grease and line with greased greaseproof paper the base of an 8 inch (20 cm) sandwich tin.

Put all the ingredients in a large bowl and beat well for 2 to 3 minutes until they are well blended. Spread the mixture evenly in the tin and then bake for about 40 minutes until the brownie is firm in the centre and has shrunk from the sides of the tin.

Cool slightly. Cut into 12 wedges while still warm. Turn out and leave to cool on a wire rack.

Makes 12 mincemeat brownies

Honey Fruit Fingers

The mincemeat filling in these fingers gives them a lovely flavour.
The baked mixture may also be cut into large pieces and served as
a pudding.

Making time about 10 minutes
Baking time about 40 minutes

4 oz (100 g) plain flour
1 level teaspoon baking powder
3 oz (75 g) spread for baking
2 oz (50 g) caster sugar
3 oz (75 g) quick porridge oats
2 level tablespoons thick honey
about 4 tablespoons mincemeat

Heat the oven to 180°c/160Fan/Gas 4 and grease a 7 inch (17.5
cm) square tin.

Place all the ingredients in a bowl, except for the mincemeat, and
mix well to form a dough. Turn onto a lightly floured table, knead
until smooth and then divide the mixture in half. Roll or press out
one piece and place it in the tin, then cover it with mincemeat.
Roll out the other piece of dough and put it in the tin over the
mincemeat. Press down lightly.

Bake in the oven for about 40 minutes until golden brown. Leave
to cool in the tin for 20 minutes, then mark into 10 fingers and set
aside to finish cooling in the tin.

If liked, the top may be covered with a little glacé icing.

Makes 10 fingers

Strawberry Cream Tarts

If you have a glut of raspberries they may be used in this recipe instead of strawberries. These little tarts are delicious to eat, sitting outside, at a special summer coffee party.

Making time about 15 minutes
Baking time about 15 minutes

8 oz (227 g) packet shortcrust pastry, thawed
½ pint (150 ml) double cream
8 oz (225 g) strawberries
3 tablespoons redcurrant jelly

Heat the oven to 190°c/170Fan/Gas 5.

Roll out the pastry on a lightly floured surface and cut it into 9 circles with a 3 inch (7.5 cm) fluted cutter and use them to line deep patty tins. Prick and then chill them for about 15 minutes.

Line each tart with a small piece of greaseproof paper, weight with beans and then bake them for 10 minutes. Remove the beans and paper and bake for a further 5 minutes. Leave to cool on a wire rack.

Whisk the cream until it forms soft peaks and divide it between the pastry cases. Arrange the strawberries on top; if they are very big, cut them in half and place them cut side down.

Melt the redcurrant jelly over a low heat in a small pan, stirring occasionally, until smooth. Spoon over the tarts. Leave to set.

Makes 9 tarts

Macaroons

Rice paper is not always easy to buy so use non-stick silicone paper instead. This paper is ideal for any biscuits with a high sugar content and the paper may be reused many times.

Making time about 10 minutes
Baking time about 25 minutes

whites of 2 large eggs
4 oz (100 g) ground almonds
6 oz (175 g) caster sugar
1 oz (25 g) ground rice
a few drops of almond essence
8 blanched almonds halved

Heat the oven to 150°c/130Fan/Gas 2. Line two baking sheets with rice paper or non-stick silicone paper.

Place about 1 teaspoonful of the egg white on one side in a small bowl and then whisk the remaining egg whites with an electric or rotary hand whisk until they form soft peaks. Fold in the ground almonds, sugar, ground rice and almond essence.

Put heaped teaspoonfuls of the mixture, well spaced, on the two baking sheets and smooth them out with the back of a spoon to form circles. Place a halved blanched almond in the centre of each. Finally, brush the almonds and tops of the macaroons with a little of the reserved egg white.

Bake in the oven for about 25 minutes until the macaroons are a pale golden brown. Take them from the oven and leave to cool slightly before removing from the baking sheets. If rice paper has been used, remove any excess paper from around the edges and then leave to cool completely.

Makes 16 macaroons

Orange Fruit Crunch

Ideal to include in a lunch box or served warm, as a pudding, with ice cream.

Making time about 20 minutes
Baking time about 40 minutes

1 orange
2 oz (50 g) stoned dates
1 oz (25 g) seedless raisins
4 oz (100 g) quick porridge oats
1½ oz (40 g) plain flour
1½ (40 g) demerara sugar
3 oz (75 g) spread for baking

Heat the oven to 190°c/170Fan/Gas 5 and grease a 7 inch (17.5 cm) square tin.

Grate the rind and squeeze the juice from the orange. Put the rind in a bowl and make up the orange juice to ¼ pint (150 ml) with water and put it in a small saucepan.

Either chop the dates or cut them up small with a pair of scissors, add to the pan with the raisins and cook gently until the mixture is thick – this will take about 10 minutes. Turn the mixture out onto a flat plate, spread it out and leave to cool.

Meanwhile add the oats, flour and sugar to the rind in the bowl and rub in the spread. Press half the mixture into the tin, cover with the fruit and then sprinkle the remaining mixture on top. Press down lightly and then bake in the oven for 40 minutes.

Leave to cool in the tin for 20 minutes, then mark into 8 fingers and leave in the tin to cool completely.

Makes 8 pieces of fruit crunch

Hazelnut Pieces

The crunchy topping sinks slightly into the cake during baking and gives a lovely flavour to a simple sponge mixture.

Making time about 10 minutes
Baking time about 30 minutes

Topping
2 oz (50 g) butter
6 oz (175 g) demerara sugar
2 level teaspoons cinnamon
3 level tablespoons plain flour
2 oz (50 g) chopped roasted hazelnuts

Cake
4 oz (100 g) spread for baking
4 oz (100 g) caster sugar
2 eggs
6 oz (175 g) self-raising flour

Heat the oven to 180°c/160Fan/Gas 4. Grease and line with greased greaseproof paper the base of a 7 × 11 inch (11.5 × 27.5 cm) tin.

First make the topping: melt the butter in a small saucepan, remove from the heat and then add the remaining topping ingredients. Leave to cool while making the cake.

For the cake, put all the ingredients in a large bowl and beat well for 2 to 3 minutes until the mixture is well blended and then spread it in the base of the tin.

Cover with the topping and then bake in the oven for about 30 minutes until the mixture is well risen and has shrunk from the sides of the tin.

Leave to cool in the tin and, when cold, mark into 18 pieces. Lift out and store in an airtight tin.

Makes 18 hazelnut pieces

Bramley Apple Slices

Serve warm from the oven. If you like spice, add 1 level teaspoon of mixed spice or cinnamon to the sugar and apple.

Making time about 15 minutes
Baking time about 35 to 40 minutes

10 oz (275 g) plain flour
1½ level teaspoons baking powder
5 oz (150 g) butter
5 oz (150 g) light soft brown sugar
1 lb (450 g) cooking apples
1 egg
3 tablespoons milk
a little demerara sugar

Heat the oven to 200°c/180Fan/Gas 6 and well grease a tin 11 × 7 × 1 inch (27.5 × 17.5 × 2.5 cm).

Put the flour and baking powder in a bowl. Add the butter, cut into small pieces, and rub in with the fingertips until the mixture resembles fine breadcrumbs. Then stir in the sugar.

Peel, core and finely chop the apples and add to the bowl. Blend the egg with the milk and stir into the mixture until it is well blended. Then spread it into the tin and smooth the top.

Bake in the oven for 35 to 40 minutes or until well risen and golden brown. Remove from the oven and, while still hot, sprinkle the top with demerara sugar. Leave to cool in the tin, then cut into 16 fingers and serve fresh.

Makes 16 apple slices

Date Shortcake

This is very good, with a crisp eating apple, as part of a packed lunch.

Making time about 10 minutes
Baking time about 30 to 40 minutes

8 oz (275 g) plain flour
1 level teaspoon baking powder
6 oz (175 g) spread for baking
4 oz (100 g) light soft brown sugar
4 oz (100 g) stoned dates, chopped

Heat the oven to 180°c/160Fan/Gas 4 and lightly grease a shallow tin, 11 × 7 inches (27.5 × 17.5 cm).

Put the flour and baking powder in a bowl and rub in the spread. Stir in the sugar and dates and knead the mixture until well blended and then press into the tin, making sure that the mixture is evenly spread. Bake in the oven for about 30 minutes until firm and brown round the edges.

Cut into 16 fingers and then leave to cool in the tin. If liked, serve the shortcake dusted with a little caster sugar.

Makes 16 shortcake fingers

Chewy Date Bars

These are so good – ideal to pop into a lunch box.

Making time about 5 minutes
Baking time about 20 to 25 minutes

4 oz (100 g) spread for baking
4 oz (100 g) granulated sugar
2 eggs
4 oz (100 g) dates, finely chopped
4 oz (100 g) plain flour
1 teaspoon vanilla extract

Heat the oven to 180°c/160Fan/Gas 4 and grease and flour a tin
11 × 7 × 2 inches (27.5 × 17.5 × 5 cm).

Place all the ingredients together in a bowl and beat well for
about 2 minutes until blended and smooth.

Turn the mixture into the tin and smooth flat. Then bake it in the
oven for 20 to 25 minutes or until it is pale golden brown all over.
Remove from the oven and then leave to cool in the tin.

Cut into 16 bars. Store in an airtight tin.

Makes 16 chewy date bars

Just Rock Cakes

Good old-fashioned rock cakes – quick and inexpensive to make. Eat on the day of baking as they are at their very best eaten fresh. They will freeze beautifully, too, so if you know that you are not going to eat them all at one meal, freeze the remainder as soon as they are cool. If you like a more spicy flavour, add ½ level teaspoon of mixed spice with the flour.

Making time about 10 to 12 minutes
Baking time about 15 minutes

8 oz (225 g) self-raising flour
4 oz (100 g) spread for baking
2 oz (50 g) granulated sugar
4 oz (100 g) dried fruit
1 egg about
1 tablespoon milk
about 1 oz (25 g) demerara sugar for topping

Heat the oven to 200°c/180Fan/Gas 6 and well grease two baking sheets.

Put the flour into a large bowl, add the spread and rub in with the fingertips until the mixture resembles fine breadcrumbs. Add the sugar and fruit and toss together to mix. Add the egg and milk and blend to a really stiff mixture; if still too dry add a little more milk.

Using two teaspoons, shape the mixture into 12 rough mounds on the baking sheets, sprinkle with the demerara sugar and then bake in the oven for about 15 minutes or until a pale golden brown at the edges. Lift off and leave to cool on a wire rack.

Makes 12 rock cakes

Toffee Crispies

These are delicious. They take a little time to make but are really worth the effort.

Making time 25 minutes

14 oz (397 g) can condensed milk
3 oz (75 g) spread for baking
5 oz (150 g) granulated sugar
1 tablespoon golden syrup
2 oz (50 g) rice krispies

Lightly grease a 7 inch (17.5 cm) square tin.

Put the condensed milk, spread, sugar and golden syrup in a thick-based saucepan and heat through gently until the sugar has dissolved and the spread melted. Bring slowly to the boil and simmer for 20 minutes, stirring continuously, otherwise the mixture is liable to catch around the sides of the pan. At the end of this time the mixture will be thick and a rich caramel colour. Remove the pan from the heat and drop a little into cold water. If it hardens the mixture is ready. Stir in the rice krispies and pour the mixture into the tin.

Leave to cool and then mark into 16 squares and, when quite cold, lift out and store in an airtight container until required.

Makes 16 toffee crispies

Treacle Spice Buns

These are quick to make and bake and are best eaten warm, straight from the oven.

Making time about 10 minutes
Baking time about 15 to 20 minutes

6 oz (175 g) self-raising flour
3 oz (75 g) sultanas
3 oz (75 g) soft brown sugar
¾ level teaspoon ground cinnamon
1 level teaspoon baking powder
2 oz (50 g) black treacle
2 oz (50 g) spread for baking
1 egg

Heat the oven to 200°c/180Fan/Gas 6 and well grease about 20 patty tins.

Put all the dry ingredients in a bowl and then put the treacle and spread in a small saucepan and heat gently until melted. Remove from the heat and cool slightly. Then stir the mixture into the dry ingredients, together with the egg, and mix thoroughly.

Divide between the tins and then bake in the oven for about 15 to 20 minutes until the buns are well risen and cooked. Leave to cool in the tins for a short time and then lift out and put on a wire rack. Serve the buns while they are still warm – fresh from the oven.

Makes about 20 buns

North-Country Parkin

Store for at least a week before eating in order to allow time for the treacly flavour to develop fully.

Making time about 10 minutes
Baking time about 40 minutes

12 oz (350 g) medium oatmeal
6 oz (175 g) plain flour
1 level tablespoon caster sugar
½ level teaspoon ground ginger
¼ level teaspoon salt
4 oz (100 g) spread for baking
1 lb (450 g) black treacle
5 tablespoons milk
½ level teaspoon bicarbonate of soda

Heat the oven to 190°c/170Fan/Gas 5 and grease and line with greased greaseproof paper the base of a tin 11 × 7 × 2 inches (27.5 ×17.5 × 5 cm). Grease the rest of the tin and dust it with a little flour.

Put the oatmeal, flour, sugar, ginger and salt in a bowl. Then put the spread and treacle in a saucepan and heat it gently until the spread has melted. Warm the milk and stir in the bicarbonate of soda until it is dissolved. Add it to the treacle mixture.

Make a well in the centre of the dry ingredients and stir in the spread and treacle mixture and then mix very well until blended.

Turn the mixture into the tin and then bake in the oven for about 40 minutes, until the parkin is shrinking away from the sides of the tin and a skewer pierced into the centre comes out clean.

Turn out and leave to cool on a wire rack. When quite cold cut into 16 pieces.

Makes 16 pieces of parkin

American Ring Doughnuts

These are quick to make if visitors pop in unexpectedly, and are at their best if served warm.

Making time about 10 to 12 minutes
Frying time about 2 minutes

oil for deep frying
6 oz (175 g) self-raising flour
5 oz (150 g) caster sugar
2 oz (50 g) spread for baking
1 egg, beaten
about 1 tablespoon milk
1 level teaspoon cinnamon

Heat the oil in a deep fat fryer to 340°F, 170°C.

Meanwhile put the flour in a bowl with 2 oz (50 g) sugar and rub in the spread until the mixture resembles fine breadcrumbs. Add the egg to the bowl with just sufficient milk to make a firm dough and mix with a round-bladed knife.

Turn onto a lightly floured table, knead gently and then roll out to ¼ inch (5 mm) thickness and cut into rounds with a 2¾ inch (7 cm) cutter. Then, with a 1½ inch (3.75 cm) cutter, remove the centres to make a dough nut ring.

Fry the rings in the hot oil or fat for about 2 minutes, turning once, until they are risen and golden brown on both sides. Fry the cut out centres to make little doughnuts for the children.

Lift out and drain on kitchen paper.

Put the remaining sugar, with the cinnamon, in a bag and mix well and then toss the doughnuts, two or three at a time, in it.

Serve freshly made.

Makes 9 to 10 rings

Jam Doughnuts

These are delicious eaten fresh from the pan.

Making time 15 to 20 minutes
Frying time 5 minutes

10 oz (283 g) packet white-bread mix
⅓ pint (200 ml) hand-hot water or milk
raspberry jam
oil for frying
about 3 oz (75 g) caster sugar
1 level teaspoon cinnamon

Empty the white-bread mix into a bowl, add the water or milk and mix together thoroughly to form a dough. Place on a floured surface and then knead and stretch the dough well for 5 minutes until it is quite smooth and elastic.

Divide the dough into 9 equal pieces and shape each into a ball. Flatten and then place a small spoonful of jam in the centre of each piece. Gather the edges together over the jam and pinch very firmly to seal. Place, well spaced, on a greased and floured baking sheet. Leave this inside a large polythene bag until the dough is doubled in size and puffy.

Heat the oil to 340°F, 170°C, and fry the doughnuts, turning them once, until they are golden brown all over. This will take about 5 minutes. Lift out and drain on kitchen paper.

Put the sugar in a bag with the cinnamon and mix well. Then toss the doughnuts, two or three at a time, in it until each is well coated with the spiced sugar.

Serve freshly made.

Makes 9 doughnuts

Large Cakes

A wide variety of cakes comes under this heading, from the rich Christmas cake through a multitude of sponges to spicy gingerbread. All can be made simply and quickly and are suitable for any teatime occasion, whether you are entertaining the whole of your son's football team or the vicar. The only danger, of course, is that your reputation as a cake-maker goes before you and you find that all your visitors time their calls for four o'clock!

Fast Victoria Sandwich

Made by the all-in-one method, this cake is the stand-by in every kitchen.

Making time about 5 minutes
Baking time about 25 to 30 minutes

4 oz (100 g) spread for baking
4 oz (100 g) caster sugar
2 large eggs, beaten
4 oz (100 g) self-raising flour
1 level teaspoon baking powder
4 tablespoons strawberry jam
2 to 3 tablespoons caster sugar

Heat the oven to 180°c/160Fan/Gas 4 and grease and line with greased greaseproof paper the bases of two 7 inch (17.5 cm) straight-sided sandwich tins.

Place the spread, sugar, eggs, flour and baking powder in a large bowl and beat well for about 2 minutes until blended and smooth. Divide between the two tins and smooth the top.

Bake in the oven for 25 to 30 minutes. When the cake is cooked it will be a pale golden colour and the centre of the sponges will spring back into place when lightly pressed with the finger.

Turn the sponges out onto a wire rack to cool, removing the paper.

When completely cold, sandwich the cakes together with strawberry jam and sprinkle the top with caster sugar.

Variations

Orange or Lemon Sandwich

Add the finely grated rind of an orange or lemon to the creamed mixture.

Chocolate Sandwich

Blend 1 rounded tablespoon cocoa with 2 tablespoons hot water in the bowl. Cool and then add the remaining ingredients and proceed as above. Fill inside and top with white butter cream (blend 3 oz (75 g) spread for baking with 8 oz (225 g) icing sugar, sieved) and decorate with coarsely grated milk chocolate.

Coffee Sandwich

Dissolve 1 heaped teaspoon instant coffee powder in the beaten eggs before adding to the mixture. Fill centre with coffee butter cream (see chocolate butter cream on page 71 and substitute 1 tablespoon coffee essence for drinking chocolate) and top with coffee fudge icing (see page 20), whisked into a swirl on each slice.

American Chocolate Cake

A really large, moist chocolate cake that is quick to make.

Making time about 10 minutes
Baking time about 40 minutes

10 oz (275 g) self-raising flour
3 level tablespoons cocoa
6 oz (175 g) caster sugar
1 level teaspoon bicarbonate of soda
½ pint (300 ml) milk
¼ pint (150 ml) corn oil
3 level tablespoons golden syrup
½ teaspoon vanilla essence
chocolate icing (see overleaf)

Heat the oven to 180°c/160Fan/Gas 4. Grease and line the bases of two 8 inch (20 cm) sandwich tins with greased greaseproof paper.

Sift the flour, cocoa and sugar into a bowl and make a well in the centre.

Dissolve the bicarbonate of soda in 1 tablespoon of the milk and then pour into the flour with the remaining milk, oil, syrup and vanilla essence and beat well to make a smooth batter.

Pour into the tins and bake in the oven for about 40 minutes, or until the cakes spring back when lightly pressed with a finger-tip.

Turn out onto a wire rack and leave to cool.

Sandwich together with chocolate icing.

Chocolate Icing
1 oz (25 g) cocoa
3 to 4 tablespoons hot water
1 oz (25 g) soft butter
4 oz (100 g) icing sugar, sieved

Place the cocoa in a bowl with the hot water and butter and beat together until smooth and the butter has blended in.

Beat in the icing sugar to make a thick icing and then use to sandwich the cakes together.

First-Rate Chocolate Cake

A fabulous chocolate cake. If you like, this delicious cake can be made in an 8 inch (20 cm) foil container, allowed to cool in the container, and then iced. This makes it perfect to take on a picnic or outing or to sell at a cake stall.

Making time about 5 minutes
Baking time about 35 to 40 minutes

1 rounded tablespoon cocoa
2 tablespoons hot water
4 oz (100 g) spread for baking
4 oz (100 g) caster sugar
2 large eggs
4 oz (100 g) self-raising flour
1 level teaspoon baking powder

Icing
1½ (40 g) butter
1 oz (25 g) cocoa sieved
3 tablespoons milk
4 oz (100 g) icing sugar, sieved

Heat the oven to 180°c/160Fan/Gas 4 and grease and line with greased greaseproof paper an 8 inch (20 cm) round cake tin. If using a foil container, grease thoroughly.

Blend the cocoa with the hot water in a large bowl and leave to cool. Add the remaining cake ingredients to the bowl and beat with a wooden spoon for 2 to 3 minutes.

Turn into the tin and then bake in the oven for 35 to 40 minutes. When cooked the cake will have shrunk slightly from the sides of the tin and the cake will spring back when lightly pressed with a finger.

Turn out, remove the paper, and leave to cool on a wire rack.

Now make the icing: melt the butter in a small saucepan and stir in the cocoa and cook over a gentle heat for 1 minute. Remove from the heat and add the milk and icing. Beat well to mix and then leave to cool stirring occasionally until the icing has thickened to a spreading consistency.

Spread over the top of the cake and swirl attractively with a round-bladed knife. Leave to set.

Can't-Go-Wrong Chocolate Cake

A moist chocolate cake that really can't go wrong and keeps well.

Making time about 10 minutes
Baking time about 30 to 35 minutes

6½ oz (190 g) plain flour
2 level tablespoons cocoa
1 level teaspoon bicarbonate of soda
1 level teaspoon baking powder
5 oz (150 g) caster sugar
2 tablespoons golden syrup
2 eggs, beaten
¼ pint (150 ml) salad or corn oil
¼ pint (150 ml) milk

Icing
2 oz (50 g) butter
4 level tablespoons cocoa, sieved
3 tablespoons milk
5 oz (150 g) icing sugar, sieved

Heat the oven to 160°c/140Fan/Gas 3 and grease and line with greased greaseproof paper the bases of two 8 inch (20 cm) straight-sided sandwich tins.

Sift the dry ingredients into a large bowl and then make a well in the centre. Add syrup, eggs, oil and milk. Beat well and pour into tins.

Bake in the oven for 30 to 35 minutes or until the cake springs back when lightly pressed with the fingertips. Turn out on a wire rack, remove the paper and leave to cool.

For the icing, melt the butter in a small pan, add the cocoa, stir to blend and cook gently for 1 minute. Stir in the milk and icing sugar, remove from the heat and mix very well and then leave on one side, stirring occasionally until the icing thickens. Sandwich the cakes with half the icing and then put the remainder on top, swirling with a knife to give an attractive appearance.

Light Chocolate Cake

This makes a light-textured cake. It uses only drinking chocolate in both the icing and the sponge.

Making time about 5 minutes
Baking time about 35 minutes

4 oz (100 g) spread for baking
4 oz (100 g) caster sugar
3 large eggs
5 oz (150 g) self-raising flour
1 level teaspoon baking powder
4 oz (100 g) drinking chocolate

Heat the oven to 180°c/160Fan/Gas 4 and grease and line with greased greaseproof paper two 8 inch (20 cm) sandwich tins.

Place all the ingredients together in a bowl and beat well. Divide the mixture between the two tins, smooth the tops, and bake in the oven for about 35 minutes until the cakes have risen and shrunk slightly from the sides of the tin.

Turn out, remove the papers, and leave to cool on a wire rack. Then fill with chocolate butter cream and sprinkle the top with sieved icing sugar.

Chocolate Butter Cream
2 oz (50 g) soft butter
4 oz (100 g) sieved icing sugar
1 oz (25 g) drinking chocolate

Place all the ingredients in a bowl and then beat very well until smooth and well blended and use to fill the cake.

Milk Chocolate Cake

A richer chocolate cake. Use a small can of evaporated milk; this will give you enough for both the cake and the icing.

Making time about 10 minutes
Baking time about 30 to 35 minutes

7 oz (200 g) self-raising flour
8 oz (225 g) caster sugar
1 oz (25 g) cocoa, sieved
4 oz (100 g) spread for baking
2 eggs, beaten
5 tablespoons evaporated milk
5 tablespoons water

Milk Chocolate Icing
2½ oz (62 g) spread for baking
3 level tablespoons cocoa, sieved
3 tablespoons evaporated milk
8 oz (225 g) icing sugar, sieved

Heat the oven to 180°c/160Fan/Gas 4 and grease and line with greased greaseproof paper two 8 inch (20 cm) sponge sandwich tins.

Put all the cake ingredients into a bowl and mix thoroughly. Divide the mixture between the two tins, spreading it evenly. Bake in the oven for 30 to 35 minutes or until the cakes are well risen and have shrunk slightly from the sides of the tin and will spring back when lightly pressed with the fingertips. Turn out and leave to cool on a wire rack.

Now prepare the icing: put the spread and cocoa in a saucepan and heat gently until the spread has melted, stirring continuously. Remove from the heat and beat in the evaporated milk and icing sugar until the mixture is thick and then use half to sandwich the cakes together and spread the remainder over the top. Leave to set.

Chocolate Orange Cake

This lovely moist cake is made in one bowl.

Making time about 5 minutes
Baking time about 45 minutes

4½ oz (112 g) self-raising flour
½ oz (12½ g) cocoa
1 level teaspoon baking powder
4 oz (100 g) spread for baking
3 oz (75 g) caster sugar
1 tablespoon golden syrup
2 eggs, beaten
2 oz (50 g) plain chocolate, grated
grated rind and juice of 1 orange

Heat the oven to 160°c/140Fan/Gas 3. Grease and line with greased greaseproof paper a 7 inch (17.5 cm) round cake tin.

Place all the ingredients in a large bowl and beat well for about 2 minutes, until thoroughly blended.

Turn into the tin, smooth the top, and then bake in the oven for about 45 minutes or until the cake is well risen, has shrunk slightly from the sides of the tin and will spring back when lightly pressed with the fingertips.

Turn out and leave to cool on a wire rack.

Coffee and Praline Meringue

This is a very special meringue and it is not difficult to make –
although I have to confess that it does take more time to make
than most of the cakes in this book. It is definitely to be reserved
for a special occasion – such as a post-theatre indulgence or as a
dessert cake after a celebration meal. This is one of the times
when I do get a piping bag and tube out for the meringue, but, if
you do not have one, you can spread the meringue flat with a
palette knife. If time allows, make your own praline, otherwise
buy it direct from a sweet shop – you will need 2 oz (50 g).

Making time about 30 minutes
Baking time about 60 to 70 minutes

Meringue
4 egg whites
4 oz (100 g) caster sugar
4 oz (100 g) light soft brown sugar

Filling
½ pint (300 ml) whipping cream
2 level teaspoons instant coffee powder
2 oz (50 g) praline, crushed

Decoration
about 2 level tablespoons sifted icing sugar
about ¼ pint (150 ml) whipped cream
1 kiwi fruit, if liked

Heat the oven to 140°c/120Fan/Gas 1 and line two baking sheets
with non-stick silicone paper and mark two 8 inch (20 cm) circles
on them.

Place the egg whites in a large bowl and whisk them at high speed with an electric or hand rotary whisk until they form soft peaks. Add the sugar a teaspoonful at a time, whisking well after each addition. It is important if you use both caster and soft brown sugar to sieve them together two or three times in order that they are thoroughly mixed. Continue whisking well after each addition until all the sugar has been added to the egg whites.

Divide the meringue in two and either pipe it in a spiral pattern on the baking sheet, starting from the centre, or carefully spread it flat with a palette knife. Bake in the oven for 60 to 70 minutes or until the meringue is dry. Leave to cool on a wire rack and when almost cold peel off the paper.

For the filling: whisk the cream until it holds its shape and then flavour with the coffee which has been dissolved in a very little water. Then add the crushed praline to the cream and spread it between the meringue circles. Place the assembled meringue on a serving dish and dust the top with icing sugar and then decorate with whipped cream and slices of kiwi fruit.

Serves 8

To make praline yourself

First well oil a baking sheet.

Put 2 oz (50 g) granulated sugar together with 2 tablespoons water in a small heavy pan and heat gently until the sugar has dissolved. Add 2 oz (50 g) unblanched almonds and boil until the mixture becomes a very pale caramel colour. Spoon onto the baking sheet.

When the caramel and almonds are quite cold and set, crush with a rolling pin – I put mine in a polythene bag first as it prevents the praline from flying all over the kitchen.

Mocha Gâteau

This cake is always very popular with young and old alike.

Making time about 15 minutes
Baking time 35 to 40 minutes

6 oz (175 g) self-raising flour
6 oz (175 g) caster sugar
6 oz (175 g) spread for baking
3 eggs
1 tablespoon coffee essence
1½ level teaspoons baking powder

Icing
4 oz (100 g) spread for baking
8 oz (225 g) icing sugar, sieved
1½ tablespoons coffee essence
1½ oz (40 g) drinking chocolate
chocolate buttons

Heat the oven to 180°c/160Fan/Gas 4 and grease and line with greased greaseproof paper the bases of two 8 inch (20 cm) sandwich tins.

Place the flour, sugar, spread, eggs, coffee essence and baking powder in a large bowl and beat for about 2 minutes until blended.

Divide between the tins, smooth the tops, and then bake in the oven for 35 to 40 minutes until the cakes are well risen and have shrunk slightly away from the sides of the tins. Turn out, remove the paper, and then leave to cool on a wire rack.

Meanwhile prepare the icing: put the spread, icing sugar, coffee essence and drinking chocolate in a bowl and beat well until smooth and well blended and then use to sandwich and cover the top of the cake. Mark the cake attractively with a fork or round-bladed knife and then decorate it with the chocolate buttons.

Easy Apple Cake

It is best to use a loose-bottomed cake tin for this cake as it is often difficult to turn out. If you do not have one, line the base of an ordinary tin with foil or greaseproof paper and carefully turn out the cake, after allowing it to cool for 15 minutes, onto a flat plate. Then peel off the foil or paper and reverse the cake onto another plate.

Making time about 15 minutes
Baking time about 1¼ hours

1 lb (450 g) cooking apples
6 oz (175 g) self-raising flour
1 level teaspoon baking powder
6 oz (175 g) caster sugar
2 eggs
½ teaspoon almond essence
4 oz (100 g) butter, melted
caster sugar to sprinkle over

Heat the oven to 180°c/160Fan/Gas 4 and line, with greased greaseproof paper an 8 inch (20 cm) loose-bottomed cake tin.

Peel, core and thinly slice the apples and put them in a bowl of water. Put the flour and baking powder in a bowl with the sugar. Beat the eggs and essence together and stir them into the flour, together with the melted butter, and mix well. Spread half this mixture into the tin.

Drain and dry the apples on kitchen paper and arrange them on the cake mixture. Top with the rest of the mixture; this is not very easy to spread but if the apples show through it does not matter too much.

Bake the cake in the oven for 1¼ hours until it is golden and slightly shrunk from the sides of the tin. Leave to cool for 15 minutes and then turn out and remove the paper. Sift over the caster sugar and then serve warm with cream.

Apple and Orange Cake

Best eaten on the day that it is made. You can serve it, with a dollop of cream, as an easy pud. Ring the changes with this recipe by using any flavour of pie filling that is handy in the larder.

Making time about 10 minutes
Baking time about 40 minutes

4 oz (100 g) spread for baking
4 oz (100 g) caster sugar
2 eggs
4 oz (100 g) self-raising flour
1 level teaspoon baking powder
grated rind of 1 small orange
2 tablespoons orange juice
13½ oz (383 g) can apple-pie filling
demerara sugar

Heat the oven to 180°c/160Fan/Gas 4 and grease and line, with greased greaseproof paper, the base of a tin 11 × 7 × 2 inches (27.5 × 17.5 × 5 cm).

Place all the ingredients, except the pie filling and demerara sugar, in a large bowl and mix thoroughly for a minute until well blended. Spread half of the mixture over the base of the tin and then cover with the pie filling. Spread over the remaining sponge mixture – do not worry if this is not very even as it will level out during cooking.

Bake in the oven for 20 minutes and then sprinkle the top with demerara sugar and return to the oven for a further 20 minutes or until the sponge is golden brown and has shrunk from the edge of the tin. Leave to cool in the tin and then serve warm – with a cake fork and some thick cream.

Serves 12 to 14

Apple and Sultana Dessert Cake

A lovely cake to serve for a special occasion. It is best tackled with a cake fork.

Making time about 15 minutes
Baking time about 1 to 1¼ hours

2½ oz (62 g) butter
1 large egg
4 oz (100 g) caster sugar
½ teaspoon almond essence
4 oz (100 g) self-raising flour
scant level teaspoon baking powder
12 oz (350 g) cooking apples weighed before peeling
2 oz (50 g) sultanas
icing sugar

Heat the oven to 190°c/170Fan/Gas 5. Well grease an 8 inch (20 cm) loose-bottomed cake tin.

Melt the butter in a pan until it is just runny and then pour it into a large bowl. Add the egg, sugar and almond essence and beat well until they are blended. Fold in the flour and baking powder. Spread just under two-thirds of the mixture in the cake tin. Then, straight away, peel, core and slice the apples and arrange them roughly on top of the mixture. Sprinkle the sultanas over the apples. Spread the remaining mixture on top; it is difficult to get this last layer smooth, but do not worry as the blobs even out during cooking.

Bake for 1 to 1¼ hours until the apple is tender when prodded with a skewer. Loosen the sides of the cake with a knife and carefully push it out. Dust very generously with icing sugar and serve the cake either warm or cold. If it is not to be eaten straight away, keep it, covered, in the refrigerator and eat within four days.

Serves about 8 to 10

Special Apricot Cake

Utterly delicious. A can of apricots is added to this cake and gives it its distinctive flavour. Use the juice from the can in a fruit salad or soak sponge cakes in it for a trifle.

Making time about 15 minutes
Baking time about 1½ hours

4 oz (100 g) spread for baking
4 oz (100 g) soft light brown sugar
2 large eggs
¼ teaspoon almond essence
7 oz (200 g) self-raising flour
½ level teaspoon baking powder
7½ oz (190 g) can apricot halves, drained and chopped
8 oz (225 g) mixed dried fruit

Heat the oven to 160°c/140Fan/Gas 3 and grease and line with greased greaseproof paper a 7 inch (17.5 cm) cake tin.

Cream the spread and sugar until light and creamy. Beat in the eggs and almond essence, adding a tablespoon of flour with the last amount of egg. Fold in the flour and baking powder and all the fruit.

Turn into the tin, smooth the top and then bake in the oven for 1½ hours or until the cake is golden brown and a skewer pierced in the centre comes out clean.

Cool in the tin for 10 minutes, then turn out, remove the paper, and leave to cool on a wire rack.

Butterscotch Cake

A simple sponge with a very tasty icing on top. It is ideal for cutting into squares or pieces to serve at a coffee morning.

Making time about 10 minutes
Baking time about 30 minutes

Cake
4 oz (100 g) spread for baking
4 oz (100 g) light soft brown sugar
2 eggs, beaten
4 oz (100 g) self-raising flour
1 level teaspoon baking powder

Icing
2 oz (50 g) butter
5 level tablespoons light soft brown sugar
5 level tablespoons evaporated milk
a few flaked browned almonds or chopped walnuts

Heat the oven to 180°c/160Fan/Gas 4 and line with greased greaseproof paper a tin 11 × 7 × 2 inches (27.5 × 17.5 × 5 cm).

Place all the cake ingredients together in a bowl and beat well until they are blended and smooth. Then turn into the tin, smooth the top, and bake in the oven for about 30 minutes or until well risen and golden brown. The cake will have shrunk slightly from the sides of the tin. Leave to cool in the tin.

For the icing, place the butter, sugar and evaporated milk in a saucepan and then heat through gently until the butter and sugar have melted and then boil together for about 4 minutes or until the mixture has thickened. Pour it all over the cake and leave to set, having sprinkled the top with nuts.

When quite cold, and set, cut into 16 pieces.

Makes 16 pieces

Lemon Cream Sponge

The lemon cream filling makes this sponge really rather special. It is at its best if you use home-made lemon curd.

Making time about 15 minutes
Baking time about 20 minutes

3 eggs
3 oz (75 g) caster sugar
3 oz (75 g) self-raising flour
¼ pint (150 ml) double cream
2 tablespoons lemon curd

Heat the oven to 190°c/170Fan/Gas 5 and grease and line with a circle of greased greaseproof paper two 7 inch (17.5 cm) sandwich tins.

Put the eggs and sugar in a large heatproof bowl over a pan of hot water and whisk until the mixture is thick, white and creamy and leaves a thick trail when the whisk is lifted from the mixture. Remove from the heat and whisk for a further 2 minutes.

Sieve in the flour and very carefully fold it in with a metal spoon.

Divide the mixture evenly between the tins and bake in the oven for 20 minutes or until the top will spring back when lightly pressed with a finger.

Turn out onto a wire rack, remove the paper and leave to cool.

Whisk the cream until thick and then fold in the lemon curd and use this to sandwich the cakes together. If liked, sprinkle the top of the cake with a little sieved icing sugar before serving.

Special Cherry Cake

A classic cake. It is important to cut the cherries up and then wash and dry them thoroughly so that all moisture is removed.

Making time about 15 minutes
Baking time about 1¼ hours

6 oz (175 g) glacé cherries
8 oz (225 g) self-raising flour
6 oz (175 g) spread for baking
6 oz (175 g) caster sugar
finely grated rind of 1 lemon
2 oz (50 g) ground almonds
three large eggs

Heat the oven to 180°c/160Fan/Gas 4 and grease and line with greased greaseproof paper a 7 inch (17.5 cm) round cake tin.

Cut each cherry into quarters, put in a sieve and rinse under running water. Drain well and dry very thoroughly on absorbent kitchen paper.

Place all the remaining ingredients in a large bowl and beat well for 1 minute and then lightly fold in the cherries. The mixture will be fairly stiff which will help to keep the cherries evenly suspended in the cake while it is baking.

Turn into the prepared tin and bake in the oven for about 1¼ hours or until a warm skewer inserted in the centre comes out clean.

Leave to cool in the tin for 10 minutes then turn out and finish cooling on a wire rack. Store in an airtight tin.

Variation

Madeira Cake

Make as above, but omit the cherries and, for a really good flavour, use soft butter. If liked, a slice of citron peel may be placed on top of the cake after the first 30 minutes of cooking time.

Mandarin Cream Gâteau

Sometimes it is nice to serve a cake like this, full of cream and fruit, for a special coffee morning. If liked, it is easy to use fresh fruit such as raspberries or small whole strawberries in place of the mandarins.

Making time about 20 minutes
Baking time about 30 minutes

4 oz (100 g) spread for baking
4 oz (100 g) caster sugar
4 oz (100 g) self-raising flour
1 level teaspoon baking powder
2 eggs
grated rind of 1 small orange
1 tablespoon orange juice

Filling
11 oz (312 g) can mandarin oranges
¼ pint (150 ml) double cream

Heat the oven to 180°c/160Fan/Gas 4 and grease and line with greased greaseproof paper the bases of two 7 inch (17.5 cm) sandwich tins.

Put all the cake ingredients in a bowl and beat well for 2 minutes until they are blended and smooth. Divide the mixture between the two cake tins, making sure that the surfaces are level. Bake in the oven for about 30 minutes or until the cakes are well risen and a pale golden brown. The centre of the sponge will spring back when pressed with the fingertips.

Turn out, remove the circles of paper, and leave to cool on a wire rack.

Thoroughly drain the mandarins; use the juice when next making a jelly or trifle.

Whisk the cream until it forms soft peaks.

Place one of the sponge cakes on a serving plate and cover it with the cream, making a slight mound in the centre of the cake. Cover with the mandarins, leaving a 1 inch (2.5 cm) border around the edge.

Cut the remaining sponge cake into 6 even wedges and arrange these on top of the cake. The domed surface will cause the points to stand up in the centre, showing the mandarins. The outside of the slice of cake is held in place by the cream.

Serves 6

Superb Carrot Cake

America has gone mad on carrot cakes. This is gooey and delicious.

Making time about 10 minutes
Baking time about 1¼ hours

8 oz (225 g) self-raising flour
2 level teaspoons baking powder
5 oz (150 g) light soft brown sugar
2 oz (50 g) walnuts, chopped
4 oz (100 g) carrots, washed, trimmed and grated
2 ripe bananas, mashed
2 eggs
¼ pint (150 ml) salad or corn oil

Heat the oven to 180°c/160Fan/Gas 4. Grease and line an 8 inch (20 cm) round cake tin with a circle of greased greaseproof paper.

Sift together the flour and baking powder into a large bowl and stir in the sugar. Add the nuts, carrot and bananas and mix lightly. Then make a well in the centre, add the eggs and oil and beat well until blended.

Turn into the tin and bake in the oven for about 1¼ hours until the cake is golden brown, and is shrinking slightly from the sides of the tin. A warm skewer pierced into the centre should come out clean. Turn out, remove the paper, and leave to cool on a wire rack.

Topping

3 oz (75 g) soft butter or spread for baking
3 oz (75 g) rich cream cheese
6 oz (175 g) icing sugar, sieved
½ teaspoon vanilla extract

Place all the ingredients together in a bowl and beat well until blended and smooth. Spread over the cake and rough up with a fork. Leave in a cool place to harden slightly before serving.

Orange Marshmallow Cake

Marshmallows give a lovely topping to this cake. Arrange them on the cake as soon as it comes out of the oven so that they soften and stick to the cake, then, when quite cold, pour over the icing.

Making time about 10 minutes
Baking time about 50 minutes

4 oz (100 g) spread for baking
4 oz (100 g) caster sugar
4 oz (100 g) self-raising flour
1 level teaspoon baking powder
2 eggs
grated rind of 1 orange

Topping
about 3 oz (75 g) marshmallows

Icing
6 oz (175 g) icing sugar, sieved
about 3 tablespoons warm orange juice

Heat the oven to 180°c/160Fan/Gas 4 and grease and line with greased greaseproof paper an 8 inch (20 cm) loose-bottomed cake tin.

Place all the cake ingredients in a bowl and mix thoroughly for 2 to 3 minutes and then turn into the tin and smooth the top. Bake in the oven for about 50 minutes or until well risen and golden brown. The cake will have shrunk slightly from the sides of the tin and the top will spring back when pressed with the finger.

While the cake is cooking, cut the marshmallows in half horizontally with a pair of sharp scissors. As soon as the cake is cooked, remove it from the oven and place the marshmallows over the top, cut side down, and then leave in the tin until the cake it quite cold.

Meanwhile blend the icing sugar and orange juice together. Lift the cake from the tin, remove the paper, and place on a serving plate. Then pour the icing over the top. It will run away into any cracks in the marshmallow topping and slightly down the sides.

Swiss Roll

Home-made Swiss Roll is not difficult to make if you follow these instructions and if you weigh all the ingredients accurately.

Making time about 15 minutes
Baking time about 10 minutes

3 size 2 eggs, at room temperature
3 oz (75 g) caster sugar, warmed
3 oz (75 g) self-raising flour

Filling
caster sugar
about 4 tablespoons raspberry jam

Heat the oven to 220°c/200Fan/Gas 7 and grease and line with greased greaseproof paper, a Swiss Roll tin 13 × 9 inches (32.4 × 22.5 cm).

Whisk the eggs and sugar together in a large bowl until the mixture is light and creamy and the whisk will leave a trail when lifted out. Sieve the flour and carefully fold it, with a metal spoon, into the mixture.

Turn the mixture into the tin and give it a gentle shake, or smooth level with the back of the spoon, so that the mixture finds its own level, making sure that it is spread evenly into the corners.

Bake in the oven for about 10 minutes until the sponge is golden brown and begins to shrink from the edges of the tin.

While the cake is cooking, cut out a piece of greaseproof paper a little bigger than the tin and sprinkle it with caster sugar.

Heat the jam in a small pan until it is of a consistency that is just easy to spread: if it is too hot the jam will soak into the sponge.

Invert the cake onto the sugared paper. Quickly loosen the paper on the bottom of the cake and peel it off. To make rolling easier, trim all four edges of the sponge and make a score mark 1 inch (2.5 cm) in from the rolling edge, being careful not to cut right through. Spread the cake with jam, taking it almost to the edges. Fold the narrow strip created by the score mark down onto the jam and begin rolling, using the paper to keep a firm roll.

Leave for a few minutes with the paper still around it so that it will settle. Lift the Swiss Roll onto a wire rack, remove the paper and sprinkle with more sugar and leave to cool.

Raspberry Cream Pavlova

This is really not difficult and does not take too long to make. It needs just an hour, undisturbed, in the oven. You must then turn off the heat and forget it until it is quite cold; do not open the oven door and peep.

Making time about 10 minutes
Baking time 60 minutes

3 egg whites
6 oz (175 g) caster sugar
1 teaspoon vinegar
1 level teaspoon cornflour
½ pint (300 ml) whipped whipping cream
8 oz (225 g) fresh raspberries
a little caster sugar to sweeten

Lay a sheet of silicone paper on a baking tray and mark an 8 inch (20 cm) circle on it. Heat the oven to 160°c/140Fan/ Gas 3.

Whisk the eggs whites, with a hand rotary or an electric whisk, until they are stiff. Then whisk in the sugar a teaspoonful at a time. Blend the vinegar with the cornflour and whisk it into the egg whites with the last spoonful of sugar.

Spread the meringue out to cover the circle on the baking tray – building up the sides so that they are higher than the centre.

Put the meringue case in the middle of the oven, turn the heat down to 150°c/130Fan/Gas 2, and bake for 1 hour. The pavlova will be a pale creamy colour rather than white. Turn the oven off and leave the pavlova undisturbed to become quite cold. Lift off the paper and then place on a serving dish.

Put the cream and the raspberries in a bowl, lightly fold them together and then add a little sugar to sweeten to taste. Pile cream and raspberry mixture into the centre of the pavlova and leave to stand for 1 hour in a cool place or refrigerator before serving.

Serves 6

Foolproof Genoese

A Genoese cake can prove tricky if you make it by adding melted butter after the flour; more often than not the mixture separates and you end up with a flat sponge. I have used this recipe for many years and find it beautifully light and moist. We like it best filled with whipped cream and soft fruit.

Making time about 20 minutes
Baking time about 35 to 40 minutes

3 eggs
3 oz (75 g) caster sugar
2 oz (50 g) plus 2 level teaspoons self-raising flour
3 tablespoons oil

Filling
¼ pint (150 ml) double cream
about 4 oz (100 g) raspberries or sliced strawberries
about 1 level tablespoon caster sugar – or to taste

Heat the oven to 180°c/160Fan/Gas 4. Grease and line, with greased greaseproof paper, two 7 inch (17.5 cm) sandwich tins.

Put the eggs and sugar in a heatproof bowl over a pan of hot water and whisk until the mixture is thick, white and creamy and leaves a trail when the whisk is lifted out of the bowl. Remove from the heat and whisk for a further 2 minutes.

Sieve the flour and carefully fold it, with a metal spoon, into the mixture. When nearly all the flour is in, gradually add the oil and fold it in until it is evenly blended.

Divide the mixture between the prepared tins and then bake in the oven for about 35 to 40 minutes until the sponge is golden brown. Turn out and leave to cool on a wire rack

Whisk the cream until it is thick and the mixture forms peaks. Then fold in the fruit and sufficient sugar to suit your taste. When the cakes are cold, use the cream and fruit mixture to sandwich them together.

Pineapple Upside-Down Cake

This cake always looks and tastes good and is delicious if served warm at a coffee morning.

Making time about 12 to 15 minutes
Baking time about 25 minutes

Cake
3 oz (75 g) self-raising flour
3 oz (75 g) spread for baking
3 oz (75 g) caster sugar
1 egg, beaten
1 tablespoon pineapple juice
½ level teaspoon baking powder

Topping
8 oz (227 g) can pineapple slices, drained
2 glacé cherries, halved
2 oz (50 g) soft brown sugar

Heat the oven to 190°c/170Fan/Gas 5 and thoroughly grease with butter a 7 inch (17.5 cm) round cake tin.

Put all the cake ingredients in a bowl and beat well for about 2 minutes or until they are well blended.

Place 4 pineapple rings in the bottom of the tin and put a halved cherry in the centre of each ring, cut side uppermost. Sprinkle over the brown sugar.

Spread the cake mixture over the pineapple and smooth the top. Then bake in the oven for about 25 minutes or until the cake is well risen and golden brown and the centre will spring back when lightly pressed with the finger. Leave to cool for about 20 minutes in the tin and then turn out onto a serving plate.

Serves 6 to 8

Pineapple and Raisin Cake

This is a less rich, moist kind of Christmas cake. It is best made just before Christmas, kept cool and eaten within a month. Drain the pineapple very well and keep the juice to use in a fruit salad or trifle.

Making time about 10 minutes
Baking time about 2 hours

2 oz (50 g) glacé cherries
7 oz (200 g) self-raising flour
8 oz (227 g) can pineapple in chunks, rings or crushed, excluding the juice
5 oz (150 g) butter
4½ oz (112 g) soft brown sugar
2 large eggs, beaten
2 tablespoons milk
12 oz (350 g) seedless raisins

Heat the oven to 160°c/140Fan/Gas 3.

Grease and line with greased greaseproof paper an 8 inch (20 cm) round cake tin. Cut the cherries in halves and roll in some of the flour. Drain and chop the pineapple very finely.

Cream the butter and sugar together in a mixing bowl. Beat in the eggs adding a tablespoon of flour with the last amount of egg. Fold in the flour, milk and, last of all, the fruit, including the pineapple.

Turn into the tin and place in the centre of the oven and bake for 2 hours or until the cake is a pale golden brown and shrinking away from the sides of the tin. Leave to cool in the tin, then remove the paper and store in a plastic container in the refrigerator.

Battenburg Cake

This recipe takes more time to make than most of the cakes in this book but I felt that it should be included. This makes two cakes. Use either home-made or bought almond paste.

Making time about 25 minutes
Baking time about 35 to 40 minutes

8 oz (225 g) spread for baking
8 oz (225 g) caster sugar
4 large eggs
4 oz (100 g) ground rice
8 oz (225 g) self-raising flour
1½ level teaspoons baking powder
¼ teaspoon almond essence
red colouring
apricot jam
1 lb (450 g) almond paste (see page 148)

Heat the oven to 160°c/140Fan/Gas 3. Grease and line with greased greaseproof paper the bases of two 7 inch (17.5 cm) square cake tins.

Put the spread, sugar, eggs, ground rice, flour, baking powder and almond essence in a bowl and mix well for 2 minutes. Spread half of the mixture in one of the tins.

Add a little red colouring to the remaining mixture to make a deep pink colour and then spread into the second cake tin. Smooth the surfaces and then bake both cakes in the oven for 35 to 40 minutes until they have shrunk slightly from the sides of the tin and feel firm when pressed with the fingertips.

Turn the cakes out, remove the paper, and leave to cool on a wire rack.

Make the almond paste as directed on page 148.

Trim the edges of each cake and cut into 4 strips as square-sided as is possible. Using the apricot jam, stick together two pink and two white strips alternately to make two chequered cakes.

Cut the almond paste in half and roll out each piece into an oblong the length of the cake and sufficiently wide to wrap around it.

Brush the top of the cakes with apricot jam and place them, inverted, on the almond paste. Brush the remaining sides with jam and press the almond paste round, arranging the join at one corner.

Decorate the top of the cakes with criss-cross scoring and then crimp the edges with the fingers.

Marble Cake

Children love this cake for a birthday or special occasion. It is not difficult to make and looks good when cut. Ice it as you like or just serve it plain and sprinkle with icing or caster sugar.

Making time about 10 minutes
Baking time about 45 to 50 minutes

6 oz (175 g) spread for baking
6 oz (175 g) caster sugar
6 oz (175 g) self-raising flour
1½ level teaspoons baking powder
3 eggs
1 level tablespoon cocoa
1 tablespoon hot water
cochineal

Heat the oven to 180°c/160Fan/Gas 4 and grease and line with greased greaseproof paper an 8 inch (20 cm) round cake tin.

Place the spread, sugar, flour, baking powder and eggs in a bowl and beat for about 2 minutes or until the mixture is blended and smooth.

Put the cocoa in another bowl with the water and stir thoroughly until blended and smooth. Add a third of the sponge mixture to it and mix together.

In another bowl put half of the remaining sponge mixture and colour it pink with the cochineal.

Choose one of the mixtures and space tablespoons of this at regular intervals around the tin. Then fill the gaps with contrasting colours.

Bake in the oven for about 45 to 50 minutes until the sponge is well risen and golden brown and the top will spring back when lightly touched with the fingertips. Turn out and leave to cool on a wire rack. Ice or decorate as required.

Family Fruit Cake

This cake improves with keeping and is the ideal type of cake to bake a week in advance and take away on a self-catering holiday or weekend.

Making time about 5 minutes
Baking time about 2½ hours

6 oz (175 g) spread for baking
6 oz (175 g) caster sugar
grated rind of 1 orange
4 eggs, beaten
8 oz (225 g) self-raising flour
12 oz (350 g) mixed dried fruit
2 oz (50 g) glacé cherries, quartered
1 tablespoon golden syrup

Heat the oven to 160°c/140Fan/Gas 3 and grease and line with greased greaseproof paper an 8 inch (20 cm) round cake tin.

Place all the ingredients together in a bowl and beat well for 2 to 3 minutes until thoroughly blended.

Turn into the tin, smooth the top and bake in the oven for about 2½ hours or until a warm skewer inserted into the centre comes out clean.

Leave to cool in the tin, then remove the paper and store in an air-tight tin until required.

Boiled Fruit Cake

This cake keeps very well if you wrap it in foil or store it in an airtight tin. It is a moist fruit cake and is ideal to cut and include in a lunch box or to take on a picnic.

Making time about 25 minutes
Baking time 1¾ to 2 hours

14 oz (397 g) can condensed milk
5 oz (150 g) spread for baking
8 oz (225 g) raisins
8 oz (225 g) sultanas
8 oz (225 g) currants
4 oz (100 g) glacé cherries, chopped
8 oz (225 g) plain flour
2 level teaspoons mixed spice
1 level teaspoon ground cinnamon
½ level teaspoon bicarbonate of soda
2 eggs

Heat the oven to 150°c/130Fan/Gas 2 and grease and line with greased greaseproof paper a 7 inch (17.5 cm) round cake tin.

Pour the condensed milk into a heavy-based saucepan, add the spread, fruit and glacé cherries. Place over a low heat until the milk and spread have melted, stir well and then simmer gently for 5 minutes. Remove from the heat and leave on one side to cool for about 10 minutes, stirring occasionally to help speed up this process.

Sieve the flour into a large bowl, together with the spices and bicarbonate of soda and make a well in the centre. Add the eggs and the cooled mixture and quickly mix together until well blended.

Turn into the tin, smooth the top and bake in the oven for 1¾ to 2 hours or until the cake is well risen, golden brown and the top feels firm. A warm skewer inserted into the centre should come out clean.

Leave to cool in the tin for about 10 minutes and then turn out and leave to finish cooling on a wire rack.

Dundee Cake

All the better for keeping for a week or so.

Making time about 15 minutes
Baking time about 2½ hours

6 oz (175 g) spread for baking
5 oz (150 g) caster sugar
3 eggs
7 oz (200 g) self-raising flour
1 level teaspoon baking powder
1 tablespoon sherry
1 tablespoon rum
1 oz (25 g) ground almonds
2 oz (50 g) mixed candied peel
4 oz (100 g) sultanas
4 oz (100 g) currants
4 oz (100 g) seedless or stoned raisins
2 oz (50 g) glacé cherries, washed, dried and halved
1 oz (25 g) blanched split almonds

Heat the oven to 160°c/140Fan/Gas 3. Grease and line with greased greaseproof paper a 7 inch (17.5 cm) round cake tin.

Cream the spread and sugar together until soft and creamy and then beat in the eggs one at a time.

Sift together the flour and baking powder and fold into the creamed mixture with the sherry, rum and ground almonds. Lastly fold in the peel and fruit. Turn the mixture into the cake tin and smooth the top. Arrange the almonds in circles over the top of the cake.

Bake for about 2½ hours in the oven until the cake is a deep golden brown and a skewer pierced into the centre comes out clean.

Leave to cool in the tin for about 20 minutes before turning out and removing the paper. Leave on a wire rack to finish cooling.

Marmalade Cake

A good family fruit cake that is always popular. Do not be too heavy-handed with the marmalade, otherwise the fruit may sink to the bottom of the cake.

Making time about 10 minutes
Baking time about 2¼ hours

6 oz (175 g) spread for baking
6 oz (175 g) caster sugar
6 oz (175 g) sultanas
6 oz (175 g) currants
3 large eggs, beaten
9 oz (250 g) self-raising flour
2 oz (50 g) glacé cherries, quartered
2 level tablespoons chopped chunky marmalade

Heat the oven to 160°c/140Fan/Gas 3 and line with greased greaseproof paper an 8 inch (20 cm) round cake tin.

Place all the ingredients together in a bowl and mix well until blended.

Turn into the prepared tin and smooth the top, leaving a slight hollow in the centre.

Bake just above the centre of the oven for 2¼ hours or until a warm skewer inserted in the centre comes out clean.

Leave the cake to cool in the tin for 15 minutes. Turn out onto a wire rack, remove the paper and leave to cool. The top may be sprinkled with caster sugar before serving.

Fruit Loaf

A fruit cake baked in a loaf tin – very easy to cut for serving and for packing in a lunch box.

Making time about 5 minutes
Baking time about 2 hours

8 oz (225 g) self-raising flour
2 oz (50 g) glacé cherries, quartered
6 oz (175 g) spread for baking or butter
6 oz (175 g) light or dark soft brown sugar
3 eggs
2 tablespoons milk
8 oz (225 g) seedless raisins
8 oz (225 g) sultanas
1 tablespoon golden syrup

Heat the oven to 150°c/130Fan/Gas 2 and grease and line with greased greaseproof paper a 2 lb (900 g) loaf tin.

Place all the ingredients together in a bowl and beat thoroughly until well blended.

Turn into the prepared tin, smooth the top and bake in the oven for about 2 hours or until a warm skewer inserted in the centre comes out clean.

Cool in the tin for 10 minutes and then turn the cake out and leave to cool completely on a wire rack.

Glazed Fruit Loaf

This is a very attractive loaf and looks good enough to sell at a bazaar or bring-and-buy sale.

Making time about 15 minutes
Baking time about 1 hour

12 oz (350 g) self-raising flour
2 oz (50 g) light soft brown sugar
2 oz (50 g) chopped walnuts
2 oz (50 g) stoned dates, chopped
2 oz (50 g) spread for baking
2 tablespoons malt extract
¼ pint (150 ml) milk
2 eggs, beaten

Topping
3 tablespoons apricot jam
a few glacé apricots
glacé cherries
4 dates
1 oz (25 g) walnut halves
2 oz (50 g) icing sugar

Heat the oven to 160°c/140Fan/Gas 3 and grease a 2 lb (900 g) loaf tin.

Put the flour in a bowl with the sugar, walnuts and dates.

Heat the spread with the malt in a small pan until the spread has melted. Remove from the heat, add the milk and then pour into the centre of the flour, together with the eggs, and mix well to a smooth soft mixture.

Turn into the tin and bake for about 1 hour. Turn out onto a wire rack and leave to cool.

To make the topping: heat the jam with a very little water and spread over the top of the loaf. Arrange the glacé apricots, with a cherry in the middle of each, down the centre of the loaf. Stone and halve the dates and arrange, with the walnuts, on either side.

Blend the sieved icing sugar with a tablespoon of water and trickle over the top of the loaf to give a criss-cross effect.

Date and Walnut Cake

This is a cake with a lovely flavour. It is ideal to include in a packed lunch and it keeps very well.

Making time about 10 to 12 minutes
Baking time about 1 hour

7 fl oz (210 ml) boiling water
6 oz (175 g) dates, chopped
¾ level teaspoon bicarbonate of soda
6 oz (175 g) light soft brown sugar
2 oz (50 g) spread for baking
1 small egg, beaten
8 oz (225 g) plain flour
¾ level teaspoon baking powder
¼ level teaspoon salt
1½ oz (40 g) walnuts, chopped

Heat the oven to 180°c/160Fan/Gas 4 and grease and line with greased greaseproof paper an 8 inch (20 cm) square cake tin.

Put the water, dates and bicarbonate of soda in a bowl and leave to stand for 5 minutes.

Cream the sugar and spread together and then beat in the egg, together with the water and dates.

Sieve the flour with the baking powder and salt and fold it into the mixture, together with the walnuts.

Turn the mixture into the tin, smooth the top and then bake it in the oven for about 1 hour until cooked. Turn out, remove the paper and leave to cool on a wire rack.

Mincemeat Cake

This is a very light, moist fruit cake and is quite delicious.

Making time about 5 minutes
Baking time about 1¾ hours

5 oz (150 g) spread for baking
5 oz (150 g) light soft brown sugar
2 eggs
8 oz (225 g) self-raising flour
3 oz (75 g) sultanas
1 lb (450 g) jar mincemeat
1 oz (25 g) flaked almonds

Heat the oven to 160°c/140Fan/Gas 3 and grease and line with greased greaseproof paper an 8 inch (20 cm) round cake tin.

Place all the ingredients, except the almonds, in a large bowl and beat well for 1 minute or until well blended.

Turn into the prepared tin, smooth the top and then sprinkle over the almonds.

Bake in the oven for about 1¾ hours until the cake is golden brown and shrinking away from the sides of the tin. Leave to cool in the tin, remove the paper and then store in an airtight tin.

Fruity Gingerbread

Gingerbread always tastes better if you keep it, stored in an airtight tin, for two or three days before eating.

Making time about 10 to 12 minutes
Baking time about 1 to 1¼ hours

1 level teaspoon mixed spice
2 level teaspoons ground ginger
1 level teaspoon bicarbonate of soda
8 oz (225 g) plain flour
3 oz (75 g) spread for baking
4 oz (100 g) black treacle
4 oz (100 g) golden syrup
2 oz (50 g) dark soft brown sugar
2 oz (50 g) chunky marmalade, roughly chopped
2 eggs, beaten
6 tablespoons milk
4 oz (100 g) mixed dried fruit

Heat the oven to 160°c/140Fan/Gas 3. Grease and line with greased greaseproof paper an 8 inch (20 cm) square tin.

Sift the spices, bicarbonate of soda and flour into a bowl and make a well in the centre.

Place the spread in a saucepan, together with the treacle, syrup and sugar, and heat until the spread has just melted and the ingredients have blended. Draw the pan from the heat and leave to cool slightly.

Stir the remaining ingredients into the bowl of flour, together with the spread mixture, and beat with a wooden spoon until smooth and glossy. Pour into the tin and then bake in the oven for 1 to 1¼ hours.

Leave the gingerbread to cool in the tin for about 30 minutes before turning it out and removing the paper. Leave it on a wire rack until it is completely cool. Store in an airtight tin until required.

Tacky Gingerbread

Chopped stem ginger gives this gingerbread a very special flavour and the finished cake looks delicious if it is iced with a simple lemon icing and decorated with small pieces of crystallised lemon.

Making time about 15 minutes
Baking time about 45 minutes

6 oz (175 g) plain flour
2 level teaspoons baking powder
2 level teaspoons ground ginger
2 oz (50 g) spread for baking
2 oz (50 g) light soft brown sugar
1 tablespoon black treacle
1 tablespoon golden syrup
1 level teaspoon bicarbonate of soda
7 fl oz (210 ml) warm milk
2 eggs, beaten
1½ oz (40 g) stem ginger finely chopped

Heat the oven to 160°c/140Fan/Gas 3 and grease and line with greased greaseproof paper an 8 inch (20 cm) square tin.

Sieve the flour, with the baking powder and ground ginger, into a bowl.

Cream the spread and sugar together with the treacle and syrup and beat very well.

Dissolve the bicarbonate of soda in the warm milk and stir into the creamed mixture, together with the flour, eggs and stem ginger. Beat well until blended and then turn into the prepared tin.

Bake in the oven for about 45 minutes until the gingerbread is risen and firm to the touch. Remove and leave to cool in the tin.

Spicy Gingercake

This is a good basic gingercake that will keep very well in an airtight tin; in fact it is better to keep it for three or four days before cutting.

Making time about 15 minutes
Baking time about 1¼ hours

4 oz (100 g) spread for baking
6 oz (175 g) golden syrup
2 oz (50 g) black treacle
2 oz (50 g) dark soft brown sugar
¼ pint (150 ml) milk
2 eggs
8 oz (225 g) plain flour
2 level teaspoons mixed spice
1 level teaspoon bicarbonate of soda
2 level teaspoons ground ginger

Heat the oven to 160°c/140Fan/Gas 3 and grease and line with greased greaseproof paper an 8 inch (20 cm) square cake tin.

Place the spread in a small saucepan, together with the syrup, treacle and sugar, and warm them together. Remove from the heat, add the milk and leave on one side to cool.

Beat the eggs and then stir them into the cooled mixture.

Sieve the flour into a bowl, together with the spice, bicarbonate of soda and ginger. Make a well in the centre and stir in the cooled milk and treacle mixture, until the result is well-blended and smooth.

Pour this mixture into the tin and bake the gingercake in the oven until it is risen and golden brown. This will take about 1¼ hours. Then turn out the gingercake and leave it to cool on a wire rack.

Store in an airtight tin until required.

Honey Cake

A simple tasty cake, that is made all in one saucepan – nice and easy on the washing up!

Making time about 5 minutes
Baking time about 30 to 35 minutes

5 oz (150 g) butter
4 oz (100 g) dark or light soft brown sugar
¼ pint (150 ml) clear honey
1 tablespoon milk
2 eggs
7 oz (200 g) self-raising flour
a few flaked almonds

Heat the oven to 180°c/160Fan/Gas 4 and grease and line with greased greaseproof paper a tin 11 × 7 × 2 inches (27.5 × 17.5 × 5 cm).

Put the butter, sugar, honey and milk in a saucepan and place over a low heat until the butter has melted and the sugar has dissolved. Then leave on one side to cool.

Beat the eggs into the mixture one at a time and then stir in the flour. Pour the mixture into the tin and sprinkle over with almonds.

Bake in the oven for 30 to 35 minutes, until well risen and the mixture has shrunk back from the sides of the tin.

Turn out, remove the paper, and then leave to cool on a wire rack. Cut into 16 pieces and store in an airtight tin.

Makes 16 pieces

Honey Loaf

This loaf is very good if it is served thinly sliced and spread with unsalted butter.

Making time about 8 minutes
Baking time about 1¼ hours

2 oz (50 g) mixed peel
12 oz (350 g) self-raising flour
1 level tablespoon mixed spice
4 oz (100 g) soft brown sugar
6 oz (175 g) clear honey
¼ pint (150 ml) milk
1 oz (25 g) lump sugar

Heat the oven to 180°c/160Fan/Gas 4 and grease and line with greased greaseproof paper a 2 lb (900 g) loaf tin.

Chop the peel very finely and place in a bowl with the flour, spice and brown sugar and stir until well blended. Make a well in the centre and then stir in honey and milk and blend until a smooth, stiff dough is formed.

Turn into the tin.

Crush the sugar lumps and sprinkle them over the top of the loaf and then bake in the oven for about 1¼ hours. The loaf will have shrunk from the sides of the tin and a warm skewer inserted in the centre should come out clean. Turn out, remove the paper, and leave to cool on a wire rack.

Light Treacle Cake

This cake has a dark colour but a very light texture. It looks very good if sprinkled with sieved icing sugar.

Making time about 5 minutes
Baking time about 1¼ to 1½ hours

4 oz (100 g) spread for baking
3 oz (75 g) caster sugar
2 large eggs
6 oz (175 g) black treacle
4 oz (100 g) self-raising flour
½ level teaspoon baking powder
1 level teaspoon mixed spice

Heat the oven to 150°c/130Fan/Gas 2 and grease and line with greased greaseproof paper a 7 inch (17.5 cm) round cake tin.

Place all the ingredients together in a large bowl and beat well for 2 minutes until well blended.

Turn the mixture into the tin, smooth the top, and bake for about 1¼ to 1½ hours, until the cake is shrinking away from the sides of the tin and a warm skewer pierced into the centre comes out clean. Turn out onto a wire rack, remove the paper, and leave to cool. Do not be surprised if the top dips a little in the centre.

Dust with a little sieved icing sugar just before serving.

German Cheesecake

A rich and moist cheesecake. If you have a second lemon rind available do use it, the more lemony the flavour the better.

Making time about 10 minutes
Baking time about 1½ hours

6 digestive biscuits, crushed
1 oz (25 g) demerara sugar
1½ oz (40 g) butter, melted
3 large eggs
4 oz (100 g) caster sugar
1 lb (450 g) rich cream cheese, at room temperature
finely grated rind of 1 lemon
icing sugar, sieved, for dusting

Heat the oven to 180°c/160Fan/Gas 4 and lightly butter and flour a 7 inch (17.5 cm) round loose-bottomed cake tin.

Put the biscuits, demerara sugar and butter in the saucepan and mix together very well. Turn into the tin and press flat over the base.

Put all the remaining ingredients into another bowl and mix well until smooth and blended. Pour on top of the crumb base and then bake in the oven for about 1½ hours, until well risen, pale golden brown and shrinking slightly away from the sides of the tin.

Turn off the heat and leave the cheesecake in the oven for a further 15 minutes. Then remove the cheesecake from the oven and leave to cool in the tin. When cold, remove from the tin and chill in the refrigerator until required.

Dust with sieved icing sugar before serving.

Serves 6

Austrian Apple Shortbread

Serve this, cut in slices, accompanied by a large dollop of thick cream. It is especially nice if served warm.

Making time about 15 minutes
Baking time about 30 to 35 minutes

6 oz (175 g) plain flour
4 oz (100 g) butter
2 oz (50 g) light soft brown sugar
1 large cooking apple
4 level teaspoons demerara sugar
¼ level teaspoon ground cinnamon
½ oz (12½ g) flaked almonds

Heat the oven to 160°c/140Fan/Gas 3.

Put the flour in a bowl, add the butter, cut in small pieces, together with the soft brown sugar. Rub in the butter until the mixture resembles fine breadcrumbs, then knead until the mixture leaves the sides of the bowl clean. Turn onto a lightly floured surface. Knead until the dough is smooth and silky and then roll out to an 8 inch (20 cm) round on a baking sheet and flute or decorate the edges.

Peel, core and slice the apple and arrange on top of the shortbread, leaving a ½ inch (2.5 cm) border.

Mix the demerara sugar, cinnamon and almonds and sprinkle over the apples.

Bake in the oven for about 30 to 35 minutes or until the short-bread is golden brown at the edges and the apple is tender. Allow to cool on the baking sheet for 10 minutes. Then transfer the shortbread to a dish and serve warm, cut in wedges, with cream.

Strawberry Shortbread

This looks very good when served for a special coffee morning. Make sure that everyone has a small fork and serve the shortbread with a dollop of thick cream.

Making time about 12 minutes
Baking time about 25 to 30 minutes

4½ oz (112 g) plain flour
3 oz (75 g) butter
1½ oz (40 g) caster sugar
12 oz (350 g) strawberries
3 tablespoons redcurrant jelly
a little whipped cream

Sift the flour into a bowl, add the butter and sugar and rub in the butter until the mixture resembles fine breadcrumbs. Knead together, then turn onto a table and knead lightly for 3 minutes until the mixture is smooth.

Roll or pat out the shortbread on a baking sheet to a round ¼ inch (5 mm) thick and 8 inches (20 cm) in diameter. Crimp the edges and leave to chill in the refrigerator for 20 minutes.

Heat the oven to 160°c/140Fan/Gas 3 and bake the shortbread for 25 to 30 minutes until it is a pale golden brown. Leave on the baking sheet until quite cold, then lift off and place on a serving dish.

Hull the strawberries, cut each in half and arrange them all over the shortbread.

Heat the redcurrant jelly in a small pan until it is dissolved and smooth and then brush it over the fruit and leave to set.

When quite cold cut the shortbread into 6 to 8 wedges and serve with a blob of thick cream.

Serves 6 to 8

Shoo Fly Pie

This rather sweet pie comes from the Deep South of the USA and is a great favourite. Serve it, cut into wedges, when you are looking for something different to offer at your next coffee morning.

Making time about 12 minutes
Baking time about 25 to 30 minutes

8 oz (227 g) packet shortcrust pastry
4 oz (100 g) seedless raisins
2 oz (50 g) light or dark soft brown sugar
4 dessertspoons hot water
¼ level teaspoon bicarbonate of soda

Topping
4 oz (100 g) plain flour
½ level teaspoon cinnamon
¼ level teaspoon ground ginger
¼ level teaspoon ground nutmeg
2 oz (50 g) unsalted butter
2 oz (50 g) light or dark soft brown sugar

Heat the oven to 190°c/170Fan/Gas 5.

Roll out the pastry and use to line an 8 inch (20 cm) pie plate or flan tin. Prick the base all over with a fork and then cover with the raisins. Mix the sugar with the hot water and bicarbonate of soda and pour over the raisins.

For the topping: sift the flour and spices together into a bowl and rub in the butter until the mixture resembles fine breadcrumbs.

Stir in the sugar and then sprinkle the mixture into the flan on top of the fruit.

Bake in the oven for 25 to 30 minutes or until it is golden brown. Leave to cool and then cut into wedges and serve.

Serves 8

Almond Bakewell Tart

This makes a delicious tart and, although it contains only almond essence, it tastes very almondy. If you prefer, make the mixture in small individual tarts but this will, of course, take longer.

Making time about 30 minutes
Baking time about 35 minutes

Shortcrust pastry
6 oz (175 g) plain flour
3 oz (100 g) spread for baking
about 2 tablespoons cold water

Almond filling
4 oz (100 g) spread for baking
4 oz (100 g) caster sugar
4 oz (100 g) ground rice or semolina
½ teaspoon almond essence
1 egg, beaten
2 tablespoons apricot jam
a few flaked almonds

To make the pastry: measure the flour into a large bowl. Add the spread, cut into small pieces, and rub in until the mixture looks like crumble – the sort that you sprinkle over apples. Mix to a stiff dough with the water; add all the water at once and mix with a round-bladed knife and then gather the lump of pastry together.

Ideally, rest the pastry, wrapped in cling film, in the refrigerator for 30 minutes.

Heat the oven to 200°c/180Fan/Gas 6 and put a baking sheet in the oven on the shelf just above the centre.

Roll out the pastry on a floured table and use to line an 8 to 9 inch (20 to 22.5 cm) flan tin. Prick the base well.

To make the filling: melt the spread in a pan and add the sugar, ground rice or semolina and almond essence and egg. Spread the base of the flan with jam and then pour the filling over. Sprinkle the top with flaked almonds.

Bake in the oven for about 35 minutes, until the pastry is pale golden brown at the edges and the filling golden brown too. Remove from the oven and leave to cool in the flan tin. Serve cut into wedges.

Serves 8

Simnel Cake

The traditional Easter cake.

Making time about 15 minutes
Baking time about 2¼ hours

6 oz (175 g) spread for baking or butter
6 oz (175 g) light soft brown sugar
3 eggs
6 oz (175 g) plain flour
3 level teaspoons mixed spice
1 level teaspoon baking powder
2 tablespoons milk
10 oz (275 g) mixed dried fruit
2 oz (50 g) glacé cherries
finely grated rind of on orange or lemon
2 oz (50 g) ground almonds

Decoration
1 lb (450 g) almond paste (see page 148)
1 tablespoon apricot jam, sieved
1 egg white
4 to 6 oz (100 to 175 g) icing sugar, sieved
small foil-wrapped Easter eggs to decorate

Heat the oven to 160°c/140Fan/Gas 3 and grease and line with greased greaseproof paper a 7 inch (17.5 cm) round cake tin.

Put all the cake ingredients together in a large mixing bowl and, with a wooden spoon, beat together until well blended – this will take 2 to 3 minutes.

Place half the cake mixture in the bottom of the tin and smooth the top.

Take one-third of the almond paste and roll out to a circle the size of the tin and then place on top of the cake mixture. Cover with the remaining cake mixture and smooth the top. Bake in the oven for about 2¼ hours or until a warm skewer pierced into the centre comes out clean. Turn out, remove the paper and leave to cool on a wire rack.

Brush the top of the cake with the jam and then take another third of the almond paste and roll out to a circle to fit the top of the cake. Press in place and pinch the edges.

Roll out the remaining paste, shape into small balls and arrange around the edge of the cake. Brush with a little egg white and bake in a hot oven at 220°c/200Fan/Gas 7 for 2 to 3 minutes to brown lightly the almond paste. Leave to cool.

Mix the remaining egg white with the icing sugar and pour into the centre of the cake, leave to set. Decorate with the Easter eggs.

Victoriana Christmas Cake

An easy, different and special Christmas cake. The dried fruit is soaked for three days in sherry which makes it very moist. This is not a really deep cake so do not expect it to rise to the top of the tin.

Soaking time 3 days
Making time about 10 minutes
Baking time about 3¼ hours

1¼ lb (550 g) mixed dried fruit, including peel
4 oz (100 g) stoned raisins, chopped
4 oz (100 g) currants
4 oz (100 g) glacé cherries, quartered
¼ pint (150 ml) medium or sweet sherry
6 oz (175 g) spread for baking
6 oz (175 g) dark soft brown sugar
grated rind of 1 lemon
grated rind of 1 orange
3 eggs
1 tablespoon black treacle
2 oz (50 g) blanched almonds, chopped
4 oz (100 g) plain flour
2 oz (50 g) self-raising flour
1 level teaspoon mixed spice

Put the fruit and cherries in a container, pour over the sherry, cover with a lid and leave to soak for at least 3 days, stirring daily.

Put the spread, sugar, lemon and orange rind, eggs, treacle and almonds in a large bowl. Sift together the flours and spice and add to the bowl. Mix together until evenly blended. Stir in the soaked fruit and sherry.

Heat the oven to 150°c/130Fan/Gas 2 and grease and line with greased greaseproof paper an 8 inch (20 cm) round cake tin. Spoon in the mixture and smooth the top flat.

Bake in the oven for 2 hours and then reduce the heat to 140°c/120Fan/Gas 1 for a further 1¼ hours. Then check with a warm skewer pierced through the centre; if it comes out clean the cake is cooked. If not, cook for a further 15 minutes. If, during the cooking time, the cake seems to be getting too brown on top cover it very loosely with a sheet of foil. Leave to cool in the tin.

Banbury Tart

Although I live near Banbury I have never managed to buy a Banbury cake there; I am told that they take too long to make. So I make it myself!

Making time about 10 minutes
Baking time about 25 minutes

Filling
1 oz (25 g) spread for baking or butter
½ oz (12½ g) plain flour
5 oz (150 g) currants
2 oz (50 g) soft brown sugar
a little grated nutmeg
2 tablespoons sherry or rum

Pastry case
8 oz (227 g) packet puff pastry, thawed

Heat the oven to 220°c/200Fan/Gas 7.

For the filling, melt the spread or butter in a saucepan and stir in the flour and cook for a minute. Remove from the heat and add the remaining filling ingredients, mix well and then leave to cool.

Meanwhile cut the pastry in half. Roll out one piece and use to line the base and sides of a 7 inch (17.5 cm) square shallow tin and then spread with the filling. Roll out the remaining pastry, damp the edges and then cover the fruit. Seal the edges well and firmly, brush the top with a little milk and make two cuts in the centre of the pie.

Bake in the oven for about 25 minutes or until the pastry has risen and is golden brown.

Leave to cool in the tin and then serve the tart cut into 8 fingers.

Serves 8

Almond Paste

To cover an 8 inch (20 cm) round cake.

6 oz (175 g) icing sugar
6 oz (175 g) ground almonds
6 oz (175 g) caster sugar
3 egg yolks, lightly beaten
almond extract
juice of half a lemon

Sift the icing sugar into a bowl, add the ground almonds and sugar and mix well.

Add the egg yolks and flavour first with almond extract and then with lemon juice.

Work the mixture into a small smooth ball by hand – but do not over knead. Divide the almond paste into 2 pieces in proportion two-thirds to one-third.

Cut out greaseproof paper patterns of a circle to fit the top of the cake and a strip to fit around the side. Lay these out on the table and sugar them with a little caster sugar. Roll out the smaller piece of almond paste to fit the circle and the large piece to fit the strip generously. For the sides, it helps to roll a long sausage shape of almond paste, and then to flatten it.

Brush the top of the cake with melted apricot jam, then put a circle of almond paste in position leaving the paper on. Turn the cake over.

Brush the side of the cake with jam and fix the strip of almond paste to the side and remove the paper. Neaten the edges with a palette knife and roll a straight-sided tin around the cake to make the side smooth. Turn the cake back the right way up and put it on a board. Level the top with a rolling pin.

Cover the cake and then leave in a cool place for 5 to 6 days to dry.

Royal Icing

To cover an 8 inch (20 cm) round cake.

1½ lb (675 g) icing sugar
4 egg whites
3 teaspoons lemon juice
1½ teaspoons glycerine

Sieve the icing sugar. Whisk 3 egg whites in a bowl until they become frothy. Add the icing sugar, a spoonful at a time. Then add the lemon juice and glycerine. Beat the icing until it is very stiff and white and will stand up in peaks.

To ice the cake: thin down just under half the icing with a little egg white. Mix to a spreading consistency and cover the top of the cake to give a smooth surface.

Put the remaining icing around the sides of the cake and rough up so that it forms rough peaks. Keep a little icing covered in a cup and then, next day, use it to fix a candle and holly and ribbons onto the cake.

No-Bake Cakes and Other Goodies

Any cake which can be made without turning on the oven must be a good thing in these days of ever-rising costs. Your refrigerator is, after all, working all the time and, unless it is very small, there must be room inside it for a refrigerator cake. Rum truffles are always popular and lend a touch of luxury to the tea table.

Atholl Brose Tart

Atholl Brose is a creamy mixture of honey, lemon, whisky and cream. The toasted rolled oats should be sprinkled on just before serving so that they retain their crunchiness. Do not expect a firm set from the filling – it should be fairly light. Each wedge needs to be lifted out carefully with a pie slice or palette knife and eaten with a fork. It is quite delicious.

Making time about 20 minutes
Chilling time about 1 hour

Flan case
4 oz (100 g) butter, melted
2 oz (50 g) demerara sugar
4 oz (100 g) digestive biscuits, crushed

Filling
3 tablespoons whisky
2 tablespoons clear honey
2 tablespoons lemon juice
¼ pint (150 ml) double cream

Topping
½ oz (12½ g) caster sugar
½ oz (12½ g) rolled oats

For the flan: melt the butter in a saucepan, stir in the sugar and crushed biscuits and mix very well. Remove from the heat and press the mixture over the base and sides of an 8 inch (20 cm) fluted flan ring which is sitting on a serving plate. Spread the mixture evenly, using the back of a metal spoon.

For the filling: put the whisky, honey and lemon juice in a bowl and beat lightly until blended and then gradually whisk in the cream, using an electric hand whisk, until the mixture is thick and holds soft peaks. Then spread it into the flan. Put the dish in the refrigerator for at least 1 hour before serving.

For the topping: put the sugar and oats on a piece of foil, place under a moderate grill and allow to brown, stirring from time to time so that the sugar blends with oats and turns to caramel. Cool, then sprinkle over the flan just before serving.

Serves 8

Chocolate Layer Gâteau

You will enjoy both making and eating this.

Making time about 30 minutes
Chilling time, several hours or overnight

3½ oz (100 g) bar plain chocolate
4 tablespoons milk
6 oz (175 g) unsalted butter, softened
6 oz (175 g) icing sugar, sieved
2 egg yolks
2 packets (32) sponge finger biscuits
5 tablespoons sherry
5 tablespoons water
¼ pint (150 ml) whipping cream, whipped

Line a 2 lb (900 g) loaf tin with foil.

Break the chocolate into small pieces and place in a bowl with the milk. Heat gently over a pan of hot water until the chocolate is melted and smooth. Turn into a large bowl and add the butter, icing sugar and egg yolks. Beat very well until smooth.

Dip the sponge fingers in a mixture of the sherry and water and place 8 of them in a single layer in the base of the tin, cover with a quarter of the chocolate mixture and spread until smooth. Repeat until four layers of sponge fingers and chocolate mixture have been made.

Place in the refrigerator for several hours or, preferably, overnight.

Turn out onto a serving dish, remove the foil and then cover with the whipped cream.

Serves 8 to 10

Fudgy Chocolate Slices

A good way of using up broken biscuits.

Making time about 10 minutes
Chilling time, overnight

4 oz (100 g) spread for baking
2 tablespoons golden syrup
8 oz (225 g) broken biscuits
1 oz (25 g) stoned raisins
2 oz (50 g) glacé cherries, quartered
5 oz (150 g) plain chocolate, chopped

Icing
2 oz (50 g) plain chocolate
2 tablespoons milk
1 oz (25 g) spread for baking
6 oz (175 g) icing sugar, sieved

Line a 1 lb (450 g) loaf tin with foil.

Melt the spread and syrup in a pan. Lightly crush the biscuits – do not make the pieces too small. Remove the pan from the heat and stir in the biscuits, fruit and chocolate and mix very well. The chocolate will melt in the heat of the pan.

Press the mixture into the loaf tin and leave in a cool place overnight until quite firm, then turn out onto a serving plate and remove the foil.

For the icing: break the chocolate into squares and put them in a pan with the milk and spread and heat gently until the mixture has melted. Remove the pan from the heat and beat in the icing sugar until the mixture is thick and smooth.

Spread all over the loaf and mark with a fork or a round-bladed knife

Serves about 8 – it is rather rich

Chocolate Juliette

This chocolate loaf is very rich, so serve it in thin slices – and offer pastry forks to your guests.

Making time about 10 minutes
Chilling time, overnight

7 oz (200 g) bar milk chocolate
8 oz (225 g) spread for baking
2 eggs
1 oz (25 g) caster sugar
5½ oz (160 g) Nice biscuits
¼ pint (150 ml) double cream, whipped
chocolate buttons, matchsticks or chocolate-coated mints to
    decorate

Line a small loaf tin, 7½ × 4 × 2½ inches (19 × 10 × 6 cm), with foil.

Break the chocolate into small pieces and place in a saucepan with the spread. Heat gently until the mixture has melted.

Beat the eggs and sugar together in a bowl until blended, then gradually add the chocolate mixture, a little at a time.

Break the biscuits into ½ inch (1.25 cm) pieces and stir into the chocolate mixture. Pack into the tin and smooth the top.

Leave to set in the refrigerator overnight until quite firm. Turn out onto a serving dish and peel off the foil. Decorate with cream and chocolate buttons, matchsticks or mints.

Serves 8 to 10

Chocolate Rockies

This is a recipe that children might like to make. Make sure that, when the cornflakes are added, they are mixed really well so that they are thoroughly coated with the chocolate mixture.

Making time about 10 minutes
Chilling time, overnight

14 oz (397 g) can condensed milk
4 level tablespoons cocoa sieved
3 oz (75 g) butter or spread for baking
a few drops of vanilla extract
6 oz (175 g) cornflakes

Place the condensed milk in a saucepan and add the cocoa and butter or spread and heat gently, stirring until all the ingredients are blended.

Remove from the heat and stir in a few drops of vanilla extract.

Add the cornflakes and mix very thoroughly until they are well coated with the chocolate mixture.

Spoon into 30 paper cases and leave in a cool place to set.

Makes 30 chocolate rockies

Chocolate Drops

These have a good flavour, are delicious to eat and keep very well.

Making time about 5 minutes
Chilling time, overnight

6 oz (196 g) can condensed milk
4 oz (100 g) milk cooking chocolate
2 oz (50 g) desiccated coconut
2 oz (50 g) walnuts, chopped walnut halves to decorate

Put the condensed milk in a bowl and add the chocolate, broken into pieces. Stand the bowl over a pan of hot water and stir until the mixture is smooth and the chocolate has melted.

Add the remaining ingredients and mix thoroughly. Divide the mixture between 10 to 12 paper cases and leave in the refrigerator until set. Decorate the top of each with a walnut half.

Store in an airtight tin.

Makes 10 to 12 chocolate drops

Mocha Bar

This is a family favourite, especially popular with the children.

Making time about 15 to 20 minutes
Chilling time, overnight

4 oz (100 g) unsalted butter
4 oz (100 g) caster sugar
3 oz (75 g) icing sugar, sieved
3½ oz (100 g) bar plain chocolate
1 rounded teaspoon instant coffee
¼ pint (150 ml) boiling water
6 oz (175 g) packet tea finger biscuits (42 to the packet)
glacé cherries and angelica

Put the butter in a bowl with the caster and icing sugars and cream thoroughly until light and fluffy.

Break the chocolate into squares and place in a bowl which is standing over a pan of hot water. Stir occasionally until the chocolate is melted. Cool slightly and then beat into the creamed mixture until smooth and blended.

Dissolve the coffee in the boiling water in a shallow dish.

Dip 6 biscuits in the coffee until they become slightly soft and arrange, in an oblong shape, on a serving dish. Spread with a thin layer of chocolate butter cream. Then dip 6 more biscuits in the coffee and place on top of the chocolate cream.

Continue layering with chocolate mixture and biscuits until all the biscuits have been used, finishing with a layer of biscuits.

Spread the top and sides with the remaining butter cream and leave in a cool place to harden.

Decorate the top with glacé cherries and small pieces of angelica.

Serves 8

Grapefruit or Orange Cheesecake

This is a delicious cheesecake to serve at a coffee party in the summer. Decorate with whole strawberries and swirls of cream. Do not forget to offer your guests a small cake fork with which to eat it.

Making time about 25 to 30 minutes
Chilling time, overnight

½ oz (12½ g) gelatine
¼ pint (150 ml) cold water
6 fl oz (175 ml) can concentrated frozen grapefruit or orange
    juice thawed
12 oz (350 g) rich cream cheese
4 oz (100 g) caster sugar
¼ pint (150 ml) double cream, whipped

Biscuit topping
2 oz (50 g) ginger biscuits, crushed
2 oz (50 g) digestive biscuits, crushed
1 oz (25 g) demerara sugar
2 oz (50 g) butter, melted
a few whole strawberries and cream with which to decorate

Soak the gelatine in cold water for about 5 minutes, then stand the bowl in a pan of simmering water and leave until the gelatine has dissolved and become quite clear. Remove from the heat, add the grapefruit or orange juice and leave to become cold and nearly set.

Mix the cream cheese with the sugar and a little of the thick, but not yet set, fruit juice. Beat well and add the remaining juice, mixing well. Lastly fold in the whipped cream.

Turn the mixture into an 8 inch (20 cm) round cake tin, the base of which has been lightly greased and then lined with a circle of greaseproof paper. Chill in the refrigerator until set. Mix together the crushed biscuits, demerara sugar and butter and spread over the top of the cheesecake. Chill for a further hour.

Dip the tin in very hot water for a moment to loosen the set cheesecake then turn out and decorate with strawberries and cream.

Serves 8

Cherry and Lemon Cheesecake

The lemon cheesecake base has a sharp flavour that goes well with the sweet cherry topping.

Making time about 25 minutes
Chilling time, overnight

1 pint (600 ml) packet lemon jelly
4 oz (100 g) digestive biscuits, crushed
1 oz (25 g) demerara sugar
2 oz (50 g) butter, melted
12 oz (350 g) rich cream cheese at room temperature
grated rind and juice of 1 large lemon
4 oz (100 g) caster sugar
¼ pint (150 ml) double cream, whipped
14 oz (400 g) can cherry-pie filling
1 tablespoon kirsch (optional)

Dissolve the jelly in ¼ pint (150 ml) boiling water then make up to ½ pint (300 ml) with cold water. Put in a cold place until the jelly is thick and nearly set.

Mix together the biscuits, sugar and melted butter and spread over the base of an 8 inch (20 cm) loose-bottomed spring mould, pressing down evenly.

Mix the cream cheese with the lemon juice and rind, caster sugar and the almost-set jelly and then fold in the whipped cream. Turn into the tin on top of the crumbs and put in a cool place until set.

When ready to serve, remove the cheesecake from the mould and place it on a serving dish.

Blend the cherry-pie filling with the kirsch and spread over the top.

Serves 8

Lemon Refrigerator Cake

A really sharp cake that needs to be made a day ahead for the full flavour to come through.

Making time about 20 minutes
Chilling time, overnight

1 packet (8) trifle sponge cakes
4 oz (100 g) spread for baking
4 oz (100 g) caster sugar
2 small lemons
2 eggs, separated
¼ pint (150 ml) whipping cream

Line a large, 2 lb (900 g), tin with foil.

Split the sponge cakes through the centre and lay a third of them in a single layer in the base of the tin.

Cream the spread and sugar until soft and then beat in the grated rind of 1 lemon and the juice of both lemons, together with the egg yolks. The mixture will curdle a little but this does not matter.

Whisk the egg whites until they are stiff and then fold them into the lemon mixture. Put half of this into the tin, then cover with another layer of sponge cakes and then the remaining lemon mixture. Finally, put in the remaining sponge cakes and press down firmly.

Put in the refrigerator and chill overnight.

Turn out onto a serving dish and remove the foil.

Lightly whisk the cream until it is thick and then spread it over the cakc.

Serves 8

Rum Truffles

This is a good way of using up broken biscuits and, perhaps, a stale sponge. The truffles are quick to make and require no cooking. Add trimmings of icing or almond paste, if you have them left after icing the Christmas cake. Adjust the recipe by adding more chocolate powder and apricot jam to bind. Make this recipe in two batches, and keep the truffles in the refrigerator or store in the freezer until required.

Making time about 15 minutes

6 level tablespoons cocoa
¼ pint (150 ml) hot water
6 tablespoons rum
4 oz (100 g) seedless raisins
4 tablespoons apricot jam, warmed
12 oz (350 g) broken plain biscuits, crushed
12 oz (350 g) madeira or sponge cake, crumbled
chocolate vermicelli

Put the cocoa in a bowl and blend with the hot water until smooth, then add the rum and raisins and mix well.

Add the jam, biscuits and cake mix together very thoroughly. Then knead together to a pliable firm dough.

Form into 2 inch (5 cm) diameter balls and roll in the vermicelli to coat the surface. Put each truffle in a paper case and store in the refrigerator until required.

Makes 15 truffles

Peanut Squares

These are easy to make and could be made by children. Use any broken biscuits that have accumulated at the bottom of the biscuit tin.

Making time about 5 minutes
Chilling time, overnight

2 oz (50 g) butter or spread for baking
1 oz (25 g) light soft brown sugar
4 level tablespoons golden syrup
4 level tablespoons crunchy peanut butter
6 oz (175 g) broken biscuits, crushed lightly

Place the butter in a small saucepan with the sugar and golden syrup and bring slowly to the boil, stirring until the sugar has dissolved and the butter has melted.

Remove from the heat and at once stir in the peanut butter. Add the biscuits and mix well.

Press the mixture into a lightly greased 7 inch (17.5 cm) square tin and leave in a cool place until quite firm. Then cut into 12 squares.

Makes 12 peanut squares

Thomas's Flan

This is a flan the children could make themselves. It is named after my elder son who makes it regularly. Decorate it with any fruit that is to hand; grapes are nice or, if it is summer, use strawberries or raspberries and in winter canned mandarin oranges look very good.

Making time about 10 minutes
Chilling time about 4 hours

Flan case
2 oz (50 g) butter or spread for baking
1 level tablespoon demerara sugar
8 digestive biscuits, crushed

Filling
6 oz (196 g) can condensed milk
¼ pint (150 ml) double cream
juice of 2 lemons
fruit to decorate

Melt the butter or spread in a saucepan, remove from the heat and stir in the sugar and crushed biscuits. Mix well and press the mixture over the base and sides of a 7 inch (17.5 cm) flan ring or a loose-bottomed flan tin. Spread evenly, using a metal table-spoon.

Put the condensed milk, cream and lemon juice in a bowl and whisk the mixture together until well blended. Pour into the flan case.

Chill in the refrigerator for at least 4 hours.

When ready to serve, remove the flan ring and then decorate the top of the flan with fruit.

Serves 4 to 6

Traffic Lights

These are very easy to make and are ideal for a children's party.

Making time about 5 minutes
Chilling time, overnight

6 oz (175 g) milk chocolate
3 oz (75 g) broken biscuits, roughly crushed
6 oz (196 g) can condensed milk
red, yellow and green glacé cherries

Melt the chocolate, broken into small pieces, in a bowl over a pan or hot water and stir occasionally until quite smooth.

Remove from the heat and stir in the biscuits and condensed milk.

Turn into a greased 7 inch (17.5 cm) square tin and smooth flat. Leave in the refrigerator until set and then cut into 8 bars and decorate with the halved cherries in the pattern of traffic lights.

Makes 8 traffic lights

Tea Breads and Scones

Tea breads spread with butter, scones piled high with strawberry jam and whipped cream – surely these are among the most tempting of teatime fare and a positive outrage to those on a diet. Nevertheless they have a place in this book because they are so easy to make and a pleasant change from standard cakes. The savoury varieties are particularly welcomed by those whose sweet tooth is not well developed.

Special Scones

The secret of good scones is not to have the mixture too dry and not to handle the dough too much. Wrapping scones in a tea towel after baking helps to keep them moist.

Making time about 12 to 15 minutes
Baking time about 10 minutes

8 oz (225 g) self-raising flour
1 level teaspoon baking powder
2 oz (50 g) spread for baking
1 oz (25 g) caster sugar
1 egg
milk

Heat the oven to 220°c/200Fan/Gas 7 and lightly grease a baking sheet.

Put the flour and baking powder in a bowl, add the spread and rub it in with your fingertips until the mixture resembles fine breadcrumbs. Stir in the sugar.

Crack the egg into a measure, lightly beat it and then make up to ¼ pint (150 ml) with milk. Stir the egg and milk into the flour and mix to a soft dough. Turn onto a lightly floured table, knead lightly and then roll out to ½ inch (1.25 cm) thickness

Cut into rounds with a fluted 2½ inch (6.25 cm) cutter to make 10 to 12 scones. Place them, spaced, onto a large baking sheet; brush the tops with a little milk and bake for about 10 minutes or until they are a pale golden brown. Remove the scones from the baking sheet and leave to cool on a wire rack.

Makes 10 to 12 scones

Variations

Golden Scones

These make a lovely change. Use light soft brown sugar instead of caster and add 1 tablespoon of golden syrup to the milk and egg mixture and beat thoroughly to blend.

Fruit Scones

Add 2 to 3 oz (50 to 75 g) dried fruit to the rubbed-in mixture in the bowl

Wholemeal Scones

Replace 4 oz (100 g) of the flour with 4 oz (100 g) wholemeal flour and increase the baking powder to 1 rounded teaspoon.

Cheese Scones

Omit the sugar and add 1 level teaspoon dry mustard, ¼ level teaspoon salt and, if liked, a good pinch of cayenne pepper and stir into the rubbed-in mixture, together with 4 oz (100 g) finely grated cheese. If necessary add a little extra milk.

Ginger and Walnut Scones

These make a pleasant change and are delicious sprinkled with a little demerara sugar before baking and then served with butter. Add 1 oz (25 g) walnuts and 1 oz (25 g) finely chopped preserved ginger to the basic recipe.

Drop Scones

These are simple to make and a great stand-by when unexpected visitors pop in at the weekend.

Making time about 5 minutes
Baking time about 10 minutes

4 oz (100 g) self-raising flour
1 oz (25 g) caster sugar
1 egg
¼ pint (150 ml) milk

Prepare, by rubbing the surface with salt, a heavy frying pan or the solid plate of an electric cooker. Use a pad of kitchen paper to do this and then grease the pan or hot plate lightly with butter. When ready to cook the drop scones, heat the pan or hot plate until the butter is just hazy, then wipe off any surplus with more kitchen paper.

Put the flour and sugar in a bowl, make a well in the centre and then add the egg and half the milk and beat to a smooth thick batter. Beat in the remaining milk.

Spoon the mixture onto the heated surface in spoonfuls, spacing them well. When the bubbles rise to the surface, turn the scones over with a palette knife and then cook them on the other side for a further 30 seconds to 1 minute until they are golden brown. Lift off onto a wire rack and then cover them with a clean tea towel to keep them soft.

Continue cooking until all the batter has been used and then serve warm with butter.

Makes about 18 drop scones

Variations

Treacle Drop Scones

To the basic recipe add 1 tablespoon of black treacle and cut down the sugar to just 1 teaspoonful. For a change, add ¼ level teaspoon mixed spice to the flour.

Cheese Drop Scones

To the basic recipe add ¾ oz (20 g) grated Parmesan cheese, ½ level teaspoon dry mustard and ¼ level teaspoon salt and omit the sugar.

Welsh Cakes

These are quick to make and may be made on a traditional griddle or in a heavy non-stick frying pan.

Making time about 10 minutes
Cooking time about 6 minutes

8 oz (225 g) self-raising flour
4 oz (100 g) spread for baking
3 oz (75 g) caster sugar
3 oz (75 g) currants
½ level teaspoon mixed spice
1 egg
1 to 2 tablespoons milk

Put the flour in a bowl and rub in the spread until the mixture resembles fine breadcrumbs. Add the sugar, currants and spice. Beat the egg with the milk, add this to the flour and mix to a firm dough.

Roll out to ¼ inch (5 mm) thickness and cut into rounds with a plain 3 inch (7.5 cm) cutter.

Heat a griddle or heavy-based frying pan and grease lightly. Cook the Welsh cakes on a low heat for about 3 minutes on each side until golden brown.

Leave to cool on a wire rack.

Do not cook the cakes too fast otherwise the centres will not be fully cooked through. Dust with icing sugar. The cakes are best eaten on the day that they are made.

Makes about 12 to 14 Welsh cakes

All-Bran Loaf

Soak the fruit overnight so that it plumps up, then, next day, all that is necessary is to stir the remaining ingredients into the mixture. It is a very easy loaf to make and the finished result has a lovely flavour.

Making time about 5 minutes
Baking time about 2 hours

12 oz (350 g) mixed dried fruit
8 oz (225 g) demerara sugar
½ pint (300 ml) cold tea
5 oz (150 g) self-raising flour
5 oz (150 g) All-Bran
½ level teaspoon baking powder
1 egg, beaten

Put the fruit and sugar in a bowl and pour over the tea. Stir well and then leave to stand overnight.

Grease and line a large loaf tin, 2 lb (900 g), with greased greaseproof paper and heat the oven to 150°c/130Fan/Gas 2.

Stir the flour, All-Bran, baking powder and egg into the fruit and mix very thoroughly. Turn the mixture into the tin.

Bake in the oven for about 2 hours or until the mixture has risen slightly and shrunk away from the sides of the tin. Turn out and leave to cool on a wire rack.

Serve either sliced and spread with butter or just as it is.

Dark Fruit Loaf

This loaf is very simple to make – all in one saucepan – and definitely improves with keeping.

Making time about 15 minutes
Baking time about 1¼ hours

¼ pint (150 ml) water
4 oz (100 g) mixed dried fruit
5 oz (150 g) light soft brown sugar
4 oz (100 g) butter
1 level teaspoon bicarbonate of soda
1 egg, beaten
6 oz (175 g) plain flour
1 level teaspoon baking powder

Put the water, fruit, sugar, butter and bicarbonate of soda in a thick-based saucepan and heat gently until the butter has melted and the sugar dissolved. Then bring to the boil and boil gently for 10 minutes, stirring occasionally so that the fruit does not catch. Remove from the heat and leave to cool.

Heat the oven to 180°c/160Fan/Gas 4 and grease and line, with greased greaseproof paper, a 1 lb (450 g) loaf tin.

Stir the remaining ingredients into the mixture in the saucepan and mix thoroughly. Turn into the tin and bake in the oven for about 1¼ hours or until the loaf is well risen and firm to the touch.

Leave to cool in the tin and then store in an airtight tin for 2 to 3 days before serving sliced, spread with butter.

Fruit Malt Loaf

This loaf is so easy (and so good) that I am sure children could make it. All the ingredients are likely to be to hand in the store cupboard.

Making time about 3 minutes
Baking time about 50 to 60 minutes

6 oz (150 g) self-raising flour
2 tablespoons malt drink
1 oz (25 g) caster or soft light brown sugar
3 oz (75 g) sultanas
2 tablespoons golden syrup
¼ pint (150 ml) milk

Heat the oven to 180°c/160Fan/Gas 4 and well grease a 1 lb (450 g) loaf tin.

Put all the ingredients in a large bowl and mix well together until a thick batter is formed.

Turn the mixture into the tin and then bake in the oven for 50 to 60 minutes or until a skewer inserted in the centre comes out clean. Turn out and leave to cool on a wire rack.

Serve sliced, spread with butter.

Banana, Date and Cherry Loaf

This is a perfect way of using up those last mushy bananas left in the fruit bowl.

Making time about 10 minutes
Baking time about 1 to 1¼ hours

2 ripe bananas
1 level teaspoon bicarbonate of soda
2 tablespoons boiling milk
4 oz (100 g) spread for baking
6 oz (175 g) caster sugar
2 eggs
8 oz (225 g) plain flour
1 level teaspoon baking powder
2 oz (50 g) glacé cherries chopped
2 oz (50 g) stoned dates chopped

Heat the oven to 180°c/160Fan/Gas 4 and grease and line with greased greaseproof paper a 2 lb (900 g) loaf tin.

Peel the bananas, put them in a large bowl and mash well. Dissolve the bicarbonate of soda in the milk and then add to the bowl, together with the remaining ingredients and mix very thoroughly for 2 to 3 minutes.

Turn into the tin, smooth the top and bake for 1 to 1¼ hours or until the loaf is well risen and golden brown.

Turn out, remove the paper and leave to cool on a wire rack. Serve just as it is or spread with butter.

Orange Tea Bread

A simple tea bread with a lovely orange flavour. Prepare it in the afternoon with the remains of the tea, leave to stand overnight and then make the bread the following morning.

Making time about 5 minutes
Baking time about 1½ hours

5 oz (150 g) currants
5 oz (150 g) raisins
5 oz (150 g) light soft brown sugar
finely grated rind of 2 oranges
½ pint (300 ml) hot tea
10 oz (275 g) self-raising flour
1 egg

Put the fruit, sugar and orange rind in a bowl and pour in the hot tea. Stir very well, cover with a plate to keep the heat in and then leave to stand overnight.

Next day, heat the oven to 150°c/130Fan/Gas 2 and grease and line with greased greaseproof paper an 8 inch (20 cm) round cake tin.

Stir the flour into the soaked fruit and mix very well. Turn the mixture into the tin and bake in the oven for about 1½ hours or until the bread has shrunk from the sides of the tin and a warm skewer inserted in the centre comes out clean.

Turn out, remove the paper and leave to cool on a wire rack.

Serve sliced, either spread with butter or just as it is.

Yorkshire Tea Bread

This tea bread is quick to make and will keep for up to two weeks in an airtight tin. Serve sliced, spread with unsalted butter.

Making time about 5 minutes
Baking time about 1 hour

8 oz (225 g) mixed dried fruit
6 fl oz (180 ml) cold strained tea
4 oz (100 g) dark soft brown sugar
8 oz (225 g) self-raising lour
1 egg, beaten

Soak the mixed fruit overnight in the tea in a large bowl, covered with a plate. If this is not possible, put the fruit in hot tea and leave for several hours or until the fruit soaks up most of the liquid.

Heat the oven to 160°c/140Fan/Gas 3. Well grease a 1 lb (450 g) loaf tin.

Add the remaining ingredients to the fruit and beat well, making a slightly wet consistency. Pour into the tin and bake for 1 hour. Test to see if it is done by putting a warm skewer in the centre; if the bread is ready the skewer should come out clean.

Leave to cool in the tin and then turn out and leave to cool completely on a wire rack.

Cheese and Celery Loaf

This is a simple savoury loaf with a delicious flavour. It is best served fresh, sliced, with butter. It is ideal to take on a picnic or to serve at a barbecue. Any left over is good toasted and used as a base for scrambled egg or baked beans in tomato sauce.

Making time about 10 minutes
Baking time about 50 minutes

1 lb (450 g) self-raising flour
2 level teaspoons salt
2 oz (50 g) spread for baking
3 large sticks celery, grated
5 oz (150 g) mature Cheddar cheese, grated
1 clove garlic, crushed
1 large egg
milk

Heat the oven to 220°c/200Fan/Gas 7 and grease a 2 lb (900 g) loaf tin.

Put the flour and salt in a bowl and rub in the spread. Stir in the celery, cheese and garlic.

Put the egg in a measure and then add sufficient cold milk to make up to just under ½ pint (300 ml), beat together and then stir into the flour mixture. Mix to form a soft dough. Turn onto a floured table and then knead lightly and shape into an oblong. Place in the tin and bake in the oven for about 50 minutes until the loaf is well risen and golden brown.

Turn out and leave to cool on a wire rack. Serve fresh, spread with butter.

Cheese Rolls

These are very easy to make and are ideal to take on a picnic or to include in a packed lunch. They are delicious served with hot soup in the winter.

Making time about 10 minutes
Baking time about 10 to 15 minutes

10 oz (283 g) packet white-bread mix
6 oz (175 g) full-flavoured Cheddar cheese, grated
⅓ pint (200 ml) hand-hot water

Put the bread mix in a bowl with 5 oz (150 g) of the cheese, stir in the water and mix together to form a dough. Turn onto a lightly floured table and knead lightly for 5 minutes or until the dough is smooth and elastic. Divide into 8 equal pieces and then shape into rolls.

Place the rolls on a greased baking sheet. Put this inside a large polythene bag and leave to rise in a warm place. This will take about 45 minutes or until the rolls have doubled in bulk.

While the bread is rising, heat the oven to 230°c/210Fan/Gas 8.

Sprinkle the remaining cheese over the rolls and then bake in the oven for 10 to 15 minutes or until they are well risen and golden brown. Lift off and leave to cool on a wire rack.

Makes 8 rolls

Hasty Spice Yeast Buns

Yeast bread mixes are handy to have on the larder shelf. This mixture makes eight substantial buns. If you do not eat them all at one sitting, split and butter them on the first day, serve them toasted on the second.

Making time about 12 minutes
Baking time about 20 to 25 minutes

10 oz (283 g) packet white-bread mix
2 oz (50 g) spread for baking
1 oz (25 g) caster sugar
2 oz (50 g) currants
1 oz (25 g) mixed peel, optional
1 level teaspoon mixed spice
a little beaten egg or milk with which to glaze

Place the bread mix in a bowl, rub in the spread and stir in the sugar, currants, peel and spice. Mix with hand-hot water as directed on the packet.

Turn the dough onto a floured table and knead well for about 5 minutes or until the dough is smooth, elastic and no longer sticky. Divide into 8 pieces and shape into balls Lay them, well spaced, on a baking sheet that is well greased. Cover with an oiled polythene bag and leave to rise in a warm place for about 1 hour or until they have doubled in bulk.

Heat the oven to 200°c/180Fan/Gas 6.

Brush the buns with a little beaten egg or milk to glaze and bake them in the oven for about 20 to 25 minutes until they are well risen and golden brown. Lift off and leave to cool on a wire rack. Serve warm, split and buttered.

Makes 8 spice buns

Quick Chelsea Buns

These buns are delicious served warm, straight from the oven, and show how easy it is to make something special with a packet of bread mix and a few ingredients from the store cupboard.

Making time about 15 minutes
Baking time about 30 minutes

10 oz (283 g) packet white-bread mix
⅓ pint (200 ml) hand-hot milk

Filling
½ oz (12½ g) butter, melted
2 oz (50 g) soft brown sugar
3 oz (75 g) currants
a little thin honey to glaze

Put the bread mix in a bowl and stir in the milk. Mix together to form a dough. Turn onto a lightly floured table and knead lightly for 5 minutes or until the dough is smooth and elastic.

Roll out the dough to a rectangle 9 × 12 inches (22.5 × 30 cm) and brush with melted butter. Sprinkle the sugar and currants over the dough and roll it up like a Swiss Roll. Seal the edges.

Cut the roll into 9 even slices and place in a greased 7 inch (17.5 cm) square tin and put this inside a large polythene bag. Leave in a warm place to rise until the dough has doubled in bulk – this will take about 45 minutes.

Meanwhile heat the oven to 190°c/170Fan/Gas 5.

Remove the polythene bag and then lightly brush the buns with a little honey. Bake them in the oven for about 30 minutes or until they are a pale golden brown.

If preferred, the buns may be glazed after baking. Turn them out and leave to cool a little on a wire rack; but serve them while they are still warm.

Makes 9 buns

Soda Bread

If you run out of bread this is a quick and easy recipe to make. It is best eaten fresh as a tea bread or as a substitute for yeast-baked bread.

Making time about 10 minutes
Baking time about 35 to 40 minutes

1 lb (450 g) plain flour
1 level teaspoon salt
2 level teaspoons bicarbonate of soda
2 level teaspoons cream of tartar
1 oz (25 g) butter or spread for baking
½ pint (300 ml) soured milk

Heat the oven to 200°c/180Fan/Gas 6 and flour a baking sheet.

Sift the flour into a bowl with the salt, bicarbonate of soda and cream of tartar. Add the butter or spread and rub in with your fingertips until it is like breadcrumbs.

Make a well in the centre and stir in the milk. (If you do not have soured milk, fresh milk may be soured by adding 1 tablespoon lemon juice.) Mix to a scone-like dough with a round-bladed knife. Turn the dough onto a lightly floured table and knead lightly. Shape into a 7 inch (17.5 cm) round and then flatten slightly and place on a baking sheet. Mark the round into four with the back of a knife and bake in the oven for about 35 minutes, until it is well risen and golden brown. Leave to cool on a wire rack.

Serve sliced, spread with butter.

Things that Children Can Make Themselves

N o book on cake-cookery would be complete without a section on cakes which children can make for themselves. Most children love cake-making and even quite small children are surprisingly skilful. Before they begin, however, do make certain that all the equipment and ingredients they need are put ready for them. With young children, it is best for safety's sake to hover nearby, partly as reassurance if anything goes wrong, but mainly to put the cakes into the oven and take them out when they are done. It is also a good plan to insist that the children themselves clear up afterwards. Many children lose interest once the business of actually making the cake is finished and you might as well teach them from the start that clearing-up goes with the job!

Chocolate Chip Bars

These crunchy bars are a hot favourite in our house. They are very easy to make because everything is put in one bowl.

Making time about 10 to 15 minutes
Baking time about 35 to 40 minutes

4 oz (100 g) spread for baking
6 oz (150 g) demerara sugar
1 egg
1 teaspoon vanilla essence
8 oz (225 g) self-raising flour
4 oz (100 g) chocolate chips

Heat the oven to 190°c/170Fan/Gas 5. Grease a tin 11 × 7 × 1 inch deep (27.5 × 17.5 × 2.5 cm deep).

Place all the ingredients together in a bowl and mix thoroughly. If you find it easier, mix with your hands. Spread the mixture in the tin and then bake for 35 to 40 minutes until it is golden brown and has shrunk slightly from the sides of the tin.

Leave to cool slightly and then cut into 16 pieces. Lift them out and put them on a wire rack to finish cooling.

Makes 16 bars

Caroline's Chocolate Slab

This recipe was given to me by a friend of my daughter. It is very popular with all my family and is an ideal recipe for children to make on their own. Any plain biscuits will do for this recipe; it is a good way of using up the broken pieces from the bottom of the biscuit tin.

Making time about 25 to 30 minutes

6 oz (175 g) plain biscuits, morning coffee or digestive
4 oz (100 g) caster sugar
4 oz (100 g) spread for baking
2 oz (50 g) drinking chocolate
1 egg, beaten
4 oz (100 g) chocolate cake covering

Put the biscuits in a plastic bag and crush with a rolling pin.

Put the sugar and spread in a saucepan and heat gently until the spread has melted. Remove the pan from the heat and stir in the drinking chocolate, egg and crushed biscuits. Mix well.

Press the mixture into a shallow tin, 11 × 7 inches (27. 5 × 17.5 cm), and smooth the top.

Break the chocolate cake covering into pieces and place in a basin standing over a pan of gently simmering water. Stir until the chocolate has melted, then spread it over the top of the biscuit mixture. Leave in a cool place to set.

Cut into 16 fingers and store in a tin.

Makes 16 fingers

Chocolate Whizz Bars

These bars are full of all the sort of things that children love.

Making time about 15 minutes

3 oz (75 g) spread for baking
2 oz (50 g) caster sugar
2 oz (50 g) sultanas
1 oz (25 g) glacé cherries, chopped
3 oz (75 g) rice krispies
4 oz (100 g) milk chocolate

Melt the spread and sugar together in a large saucepan. Add the sultanas and glacé cherries and cook for 3 minutes, then remove from the heat and stir in the krispies carefully, without crushing them. Press the mixture into a greased tin, 7 × 11 inches (17.5 × 27.5 cm).

Place the chocolate, broken into pieces, in a small bowl and stand the bowl over a pan of water on a gentle heat until the chocolate has melted. Carefully spread it over the top of the rice krispie mixture, using a large flat knife or spatula.

Leave to set until firm, or chill for 1 to 2 hours, then cut into 24 bars.

Makes 24 bars

Chocolate Krispies

These are most children's all-time favourites. For the best results they should be eaten on the day that they are made – this is usually no problem! Let the children make them themselves and try and persuade them that it is worth waiting for the krispies to set.

Making time about 10 minutes

2 oz (50 g) butter or spread for baking
2 level tablespoons drinking chocolate
1 rounded tablespoon golden syrup
2½ oz (62 g) rice krispies

Put the butter or spread in a saucepan and heat gently until it is melted. Stir in the chocolate and golden syrup and mix well. Remove from the heat and tip in all the krispies and stir very well so that they become evenly coated with the chocolate mixture.

Using two spoons, pile the mixture into about 12 to 15 paper cases. Then leave to harden in a cool room for about 30 minutes.

Store any krispies that are not eaten in an airtight tin.

Makes about 12 to 15 chocolate krispies

Milk Chocolate Krispies

These are very easy to make and store well in a tin. Children love the flavour of milk chocolate but the krispies may, of course, be made with plain chocolate if preferred.

Making time about 5 minutes

4 oz (100 g) milk chocolate
2 oz (50 g) rice krispies

Break the chocolate into a bowl and then stand it over a pan of gently simmering water until the chocolate is melted and smooth. Remove from the heat and stir in the krispies. Mix very thoroughly until all the krispies are well coated. Divide the mixture between 15 paper cases and leave to set.

Store in an airtight tin.

Makes 15 milk chocolate krispies

Coconut Ice

This is an easy no-cook recipe that children can make on their own.

Making time about 15 minutes

12 level tablespoons condensed milk
12 oz (350 g) icing sugar
6 oz (175 g) desiccated coconut
cochineal

Put the condensed milk, icing sugar and coconut together in a large bowl and mix very thoroughly until the mixture will come together and can be lightly kneaded to a smooth ball.

Lightly grease a 7 inch (17.5 cm) square tin and then press half of the mixture evenly over the base of the tin.

Add some pink colouring to the mixture remaining in the bowl. It is surprising how much will be needed to make a good pink colour – the best way to add the colour is to drip it, drop by drop, from a skewer dipped in the cochineal. Work each addition thoroughly into the mixture to make sure that the pink is a good colour all through.

Press out the pink mixture flat on top of the white mixture and leave in a cool place to set, preferably overnight.

Cut into 36 squares and leave in an airtight tin until required.

Makes 36 pieces of coconut ice

Coconut Pyramids

These are often one of the first things that children are taught to make at school – they are so simple that very little can go wrong!

Making time about 10 to 12 minutes
Baking time about 20 minutes

4 oz (100 g) desiccated coconut
2 oz (50 g) caster sugar
1 egg, beaten
a little pink colouring

Heat the oven to 180°c/160Fan/Gas 4 and grease a baking sheet.

Put the coconut and sugar in a bowl and mix together. Beat in sufficient egg to bind the mixture together and add a few drops of pink colouring.

Dip a small conical mould or egg cup into cold water and then drain it and fill with the coconut mixture. Pressing down gently, turn the mould out onto the baking sheet. Continue with the remaining mixture – it will make about 6 or 7 pyramids.

Bake in the oven for 20 minutes or until the pyramids are tinged a pale golden brown. Lift off the baking sheet and leave them to cool on a wire rack.

Makes 6 or 7 pyramids

Caramel Crunch Bars

Children love to eat these bars instead of cakes or biscuits; I find that they are also very popular accompaniments to ice cream or mousse. You can cut down the recipe and only make half quantity, but in our house they are so popular and useful that it never seems worthwhile making less.

Making time about 10 minutes

4 oz (100 g) spread for baking
4 oz (100 g) marshmallows
4 oz (100 g) caramels
7 oz (200 g) rice krispies

Put the spread, marshmallows and caramels in a saucepan and heat gently over a moderate heat until the mixture is melted and smooth. Be patient, this will take about 5 minutes.

Meanwhile put the krispies in a large bowl. Remove the pan from the heat and pour all at once onto the krispies and stir very thoroughly until they are well and evenly coated.

Spoon into a large tin, 12 × 9 inches (30 × 22.5 cm), and press flat. Leave in a cool place until set and quite firm and then cut into 21 bars.

Makes 21 caramel crunch bars

Oat Crunchies

The making of these provides ideal entertainment for the children on a wet afternoon. The crunchies are quick and easy – the main problem seems to be that there are never any left to put in a tin for another day.

Making time about 8 to 10 minutes
Baking time about 15 to 20 minutes

5 oz (150 g) quick porridge oats
4 oz (100 g) demerara sugar
4 oz (100 g) spread for baking

Heat the oven to 190°c/170Fan/Gas 5 and grease a shallow tin, 11 × 7 inches (27.5 × 17.5 cm).

Put the oats and sugar in a bowl. Heat the spread in a saucepan until it has melted, then pour it onto the oats and mix thoroughly until blended. Press the mixture over the base of the tin.

Bake in the oven for 15 to 20 minutes until pale golden brown, then remove and mark into 16 pieces. Leave to cool in the tin until quite cold.

Makes 16 oat crunchies

Flap Jacks

These are simple and quick to make from ingredients that are in the store cupboard. Most children find them very easy both to make and eat!

Making time about 5 minutes
Baking time about 35 minutes

4 oz (100 g) spread for baking
4 oz (100 g) demerara sugar
1 level tablespoon golden syrup
5 oz (150 g) rolled oats

Heat the oven 160°c/140Fan/Gas 3 and grease a 7 inch (17.5 cm) square tin.

Melt the spread in a pan with the sugar and syrup and stir in the oats. Mix very well and then turn into the tin and press flat.

Bake in the oven for about 35 minutes or until golden brown. Remove from the oven and then leave to cool for 10 minutes. Mark into 12 squares and then leave to finish cooling in the tin.

Lift out and store in an airtight container.

Makes 12 flap jacks

Variation

Dark Treacly Jacks

Instead of demerara sugar use dark soft brown sugar which gives a lovely flavour and texture.

Afghans

Everybody's favourites; children love making and eating these.

Making time about 20 minutes
Baking time about 20 minutes

6 oz (175 g) spread for baking
4 oz (100 g) caster sugar
5 oz (150 g) plain flour
2 level tablespoons cocoa
2 oz (50 g) crushed cornflakes

Heat the oven to 180°c/160Fan/Gas 4 and grease several baking sheets.

Cream the spread and sugar together until soft and then gradually work in the flour, cocoa and, lastly, the crushed cornflakes. Shape the mixture into small balls the size of a walnut and place, well spaced, on the baking sheets. Press each ball down with two fingers.

Bake in the oven for 15 to 20 minutes, lift off and leave to cool on a wire rack and then store in an airtight tin.

Makes 30 to 35 biscuits

Muesli Jacks

There is no need to use scales for this recipe. Judge the spread for baking by using just under half a block. Use a 5 oz cream or yogurt carton to measure the other ingredients.

Making time about 15 minutes
Baking time about 15 to 20 minutes

4 oz (100 g) spread for baking
1 rounded tablespoon golden syrup
1 level carton (4½ oz/112 g) demerara sugar
1 level carton (3 oz/75 g) mixed cereal with fruit and nuts
1 level carton (3 oz/75 g) self-raising flour

Heat the oven to 160°c/140Fan/Gas 3 and grease three large baking sheets.

Put the spread, syrup and demerara sugar in a saucepan and place over a low heat until the spread has melted. Remove from the heat and stir in the mixed cereal and flour and stir well.

Allow the mixture to cool slightly and then roll it into small balls and place them, well spaced, on the baking sheets.

Bake for about 15 to 20 minutes until the balls are a pale golden brown all over. Remove from the oven and leave for a few minutes to cool and slightly harden and then lift off and put on a wire rack to cool.

Store in an airtight tin.

Makes about 30 biscuits

Cornflake Cookies

These are easy to make from ingredients that are always in the store cupboard. They are just the thing for children to make when boredom sets in at holiday time.

Making time about 25 minutes
Baking time about 20 to 25 minutes

8 oz (225 g) spread for baking
6 oz (175 g) caster or light soft brown sugar
1 egg, beaten
10 oz (275 g) self-raising flour
2 oz (50 g) cornflakes, lightly crushed

Heat the oven to 190°c/170Fan/Gas 5 and grease three large baking sheets.

Put the spread into a large bowl, add the sugar and beat together with a wooden spoon until light and creamy. Beat in the egg, then slowly work in the flour until all the mixture has come together. If it is a warm day or the kitchen is very hot the mixture may be soft to handle, so wrap it in a piece of cling film and chill in the refrigerator for about 15 minutes. Wet your hands and lightly roll the mixture into about 34 balls and then coat each in the crushed cornflakes. This will take a little time but is worth doing carefully.

Position the cookies, well spaced, on the baking sheets and flatten each slightly with your hand. Bake for about 20 to 25 minutes until the cookies turn a very pale brown at the edges.

Remove from the oven and leave on the trays for a minute before carefully lifting each biscuit onto a wire rack to cool. When cold, store in an airtight tin.

Makes about 34 cookies

Jammy Buns

I asked a 12-year-old girl to try this recipe for me – she had no problems and thoroughly enjoyed herself. The buns are best eaten fresh from the oven.

Making time about 20 minutes
Baking time about 10 to 15 minutes

8 oz (225 g) self-raising flour
pinch of mixed spice
2 oz (50 g) butter
2 oz (50 g) caster sugar
1 egg, beaten
about 2 tablespoons milk
strawberry jam
a little granulated sugar

Heat the oven to 200°c/180Fan/Gas 6 and grease a large baking sheet.

Put the flour, spice and butter in a bowl and rub in the butter until the mixture resembles fine breadcrumbs. Stir in the sugar.

Blend the egg with the milk and stir into the mixture, adding sufficient of the liquid to make a stiff dough. Divide the mixture into 12 pieces and roll into balls. Make a hole in the centre of each with the handle of a wooden spoon and put about ½ teaspoon of jam into each one, then pinch the opening firmly together.

Turn them over and place, jam side down, on the baking sheets. Sprinkle them with a little granulated sugar and then bake for

10 to 15 minutes until they are pale golden brown. Lift off the tray and cool on a wire rack. Serve warm.

Makes 12 buns

Popping Pop Corn

Great fun for children to make. It is best to use a large pan with a heavy base and a well-fitting lid. Take care not to lift the lid while the corn is popping, otherwise there will be popcorn everywhere.

Making time about 10 minutes

3 tablespoons oil
5 oz (150 g) popping corn

Put the oil into a large pan which has a heavy base and a well-fitting lid, and then add the popping corn. Put the pan over a medium heat and leave it for about 3 minutes or until you hear the first pop.

Hold the handle of the saucepan with one hand and, with an oven glove, hold the lid with the other hand. Shake the pan firmly while keeping it on the heat all the time.

The popping will continue and become quite loud until it sounds like gunfire! Do not remove the lid as the corn will go all over the place. When the popping has died down take the pan off the heat, hold it at arm's length and gently ease off the lid in order to let all the steam out.

Pour the popped corn into a large bowl. Any unpopped corn left in the pan should be thrown away as it cannot be used again.

Sprinkle the pop corn with a little sugar and serve.

Variations

Cheese Pop Corn

Put the basic popped corn in a meat roasting tin and scatter grated Cheddar cheese over it. You will need about 4 oz (100 g) cheese to 2½ oz (62 g) of popped corn. Put the tin in a moderate oven for about 5 to 8 minutes until the cheese has melted and stuck to the corn. Turn into a serving dish.

Chocolate Pop Corn

Put 2½ oz (62 g) popped corn in a large bowl. Put 2 oz (50 g) butter and 2 level tablespoons drinking chocolate into a saucepan and heat gently, stirring continuously, until the butter has melted. Then remove the chocolate mixture from the heat and pour over the pop corn. Stir thoroughly so that all the pieces are well coated.

Biscuits

People often apologise for offering biscuits instead of cakes to their guests. I cannot think why. The genuine home-made biscuit is one of the most mouth-watering delicacies ever to grace the tea table. Provided that they are stored in airtight tins so that they do not go soggy, biscuits retain their flavour for a long time. In addition, because they do not crumble, they are so much easier than cakes to pack in a child's lunch box or to take on picnics.

Shortbread Finger Biscuits

This is a basic recipe that can be adapted very easily to make all sorts of interesting biscuits.

Making time about 15 minutes
Baking time about 20 minutes

8 oz (225 g) spread for baking
2 oz (50 g) icing sugar
8 oz (225 g) plain flour

Heat the oven to 160°c/140Fan/Gas 3. Lightly grease two baking sheets.

Put the ingredients in a bowl and rub in the spread with your fingertips until the mixture resembles fine breadcrumbs. Knead together with your hand until it forms a smooth soft mixture.

Place the mixture in a piping bag fitted with a large star vegetable nozzle and pipe out into 2 to 3 inch (5 to 7.5 cm) lengths.

Bake the biscuits in the oven for about 20 minutes until they are tinged a pale golden brown at the edges.

Remove them from the oven, leave to harden for a minute and then lift off and leave to cool on a wire rack.

Makes about 30 finger biscuits

Variations

Shortbread Rounds

Pipe the basic mixture into circles or rosettes. Put a blob of jam in the centre of each. Bake as above. Redcurrant jam gives a good result.

Chocolate Fingers

Make and pipe as in the basic recipe and then, when quite cold, dip the ends of the biscuits in a little melted chocolate and leave to set.

Glazed Orange Shells

Add the grated rind of an orange to the basic mixture and then pipe onto the baking sheets in shell shapes. Bake for 20 minutes and then remove from the oven and brush with a little warm sieved apricot jam. Blend 2 oz (50 g) icing sugar with 1 tablespoon orange juice and brush this over the jam. Return the biscuits to the oven for a further 5 minutes or until the glaze crystallises. Leave to cool on a wire rack

Botermoppen

These are Dutch shortbread biscuits and have a lovely flavour. This basic recipe may be easily adapted for any of the variations that I have included below.

Making time about 10 minutes
Baking time about 25 minutes

6 oz (175 g) unsalted butter
finely grated rind of half a lemon
4 oz (100 g) caster sugar
8 oz (225 g) plain flour
1 oz (25 g) granulated sugar

Heat the oven to 160°c/140Fan/Gas 3 and grease two or three large baking trays.

Cream the butter and lemon rind in a large bowl until soft, and then beat in the sugar until the mixture is light. Blend in the flour and knead lightly until smooth (use your hands for this). Then divide the mixture into two, roll out to form two 6 inch (15 cm) sausages and cover these in granulated sugar. Wrap in foil and chill in the refrigerator until firm.

Cut each sausage into 16 slices and place on the baking sheets allowing a little room for them to spread, and then bake in the oven for about 25 minutes or until they are pale golden brown at the edges. Carefully lift off and leave to cool on a wire rack.

Makes 32 botermoppen

Variations

Janhagel

Using the same basic mixture omit the lemon rind and instead add 1 level teaspoon ground cinnamon. Press the dough into a shallow tin 7 × 11 inches (17.5 × 27.5 cm) and flatten with a knife. Prick well and glaze with a little beaten egg or milk and then sprinkle with granulated sugar and about 1 oz (25 g) flaked almonds. Bake in the oven for 40 minutes. Leave to cool in the tin for 15 minutes before cutting into 16 fingers.

Demerara Biscuits

Use demerara sugar instead of caster sugar when making the basic recipe, roll the dough in demerara sugar instead of granulated and then chill and bake as above.

Chocolate Crunch Biscuits

Make as the basic recipe but omit the lemon rind and use 7 oz (200 g) plain flour and 1 oz (25 g) cocoa.

Cherry Shortbread

Cherries added to this basic shortbread give it a nice flavour and texture. This is a good recipe to prepare for a bazaar or for a bring-and-buy sale.

Making time about 10 minutes
Baking time about 35 minutes

4 oz (100 g) plain flour
2 oz (50 g) cornflour
4 oz (100 g) butter
2 oz (50 g) caster sugar
2 oz (50 g) glacé cherries, chopped
icing sugar

Heat the oven to 160°c/140Fan/Gas 3 and grease a 7 inch (17.5 cm) square tin.

Sift the flour and cornflour together.

Cream the butter and sugar together until light and fluffy and then work in the flours and cherries and knead well together.

Press the mixture into the tin and bake in the oven for about 35 minutes or until a very pale golden brown.

Remove from the oven and mark into 12 fingers. Leave the short-bread to cool in the tin.

Lift out onto a wire rack and sprinkle with sieved icing sugar.

Makes 12 shortbread fingers

Variation

Walnut Shortbread

Instead of cherries add 1 oz (25 g) finely chopped walnuts – or, in fact, any variety of chopped nuts as long as they are unsalted. You could use more if you like, but nuts have a strong flavour and 1 oz (25 g) usually proves sufficient.

Chocolate Caramel Shortbread

These are not ultra-quick to make, however they are great favourites with all ages. Do not expect the caramel to harden – it does not – and the shortbread is gooey and sticky to eat. When this recipe was given to me it had 7 oz (200 g) of chocolate on top, which I found too rich and too expensive; 4 oz (100 g) is plenty.

Making time about 20 minutes
Baking time about 25 minutes

Base
4 oz (100 g) spread for baking
2 oz (50 g) caster sugar
6 oz (150 g) plain flour

Caramel
4 oz (100 g) spread for baking
3 oz (75 g) caster sugar
2 level tablespoons golden syrup
6 oz (193 g) can condensed milk

Topping
3½ oz (100 g) bar plain chocolate

Heat the oven to 180°c/160Fan/Gas 4. Grease a Swiss Roll tin 7 × 11 inches (17.5 × 27.5 cm).

Place all the ingredients for the base in a bowl and beat to a firm dough. (The mixture may require a light kneading with the hand to come together.)

Press into the tin with the back of a metal spoon or the palm of the hand. Prick with a fork and then bake for 25 to 30 minutes until a pale brown.

While the shortbread is baking, prepare the caramel. Put all the ingredients in a saucepan and heat gently until they are melted. Then boil the mixture for 5 to 10 minutes until it is caramel coloured. Stir continuously, preferably with a flat-based wooden spoon which can get into the sides of the pan and prevent the mixture from catching, which, given half a chance, it will do! Leave to cool slightly and then, when the shortbread is cooked and has cooled for about 5 minutes, pour the caramel over it and leave on one side.

Melt the chocolate by breaking it into pieces and placing it in a small heatproof bowl standing over a saucepan of water. Heat gently until the chocolate has melted and is smooth.

Pour the chocolate in a steady stream over the caramel and, with a fork lightly make a swirling pattern. Leave undisturbed for several hours then cut into 21 pieces.

Makes 21 fingers

Almond Crisps

These biscuits are perfect to serve with mousses and fools. They seem to lose their flavour quite quickly in a tin so they are best served fresh.

Making time about 5 minutes
Baking time 8 to 10 minutes

2½ oz (62 g) butter
2 oz (50 g) caster sugar
1½ oz (40 g) plain flour
1½ oz (40 g) flaked almonds

Heat the oven to 180°c/160Fan/Gas 4 and grease about three large baking sheets.

Cream the butter and sugar until very pale and then stir in the flour and the almonds. Shape into marble-sized balls and place them about 3 inches (7.5 cm) apart on the baking sheets and flatten with a damp fork.

Bake in the oven for 8 to 10 minutes until they are a pale golden brown.

Remove them from the oven, leave to cool for a few seconds and then carefully lift each off with a palette knife and lay it over a lightly oiled rolling pin and leave to harden. Then lift off.

Makes about 18 almond crisps

Lemon Crisps

These biscuits are simple to make, have a lovely flavour and keep well in an airtight tin.

Making time about 25 minutes
Baking time about 15 to 20 minutes

4 oz (100 g) spread for baking
4 oz (100 g) caster sugar
1 egg, beaten
8 oz (225 g) self-raising flour
grated rind of 1 lemon

Heat the oven to 180°c/160Fan/Gas 4. Grease two or three baking sheets.

Cream the spread and sugar together and then add the remaining ingredients and work together until they form a smooth dough. Put this in the refrigerator and chill for 15 minutes.

Roll out the dough thinly on a lightly floured or sugared table and cut into rounds with a 3 inch (7.5 cm) cutter. (Use a fluted one if possible.)

Place the rounds, evenly spaced, on the baking sheets and bake in the oven for 15 to 20 minutes until they are a very pale golden brown and are crisp; the flavour is spoilt if the biscuits are allowed to get too brown.

Lift off and leave to cool on a wire rack. Store in an airtight tin.

Makes 24 to 30 lemon crisps

Variation

Orange Crisps

Use the grated rind of 1 medium-sized orange instead of the lemon rind and make as above.

Cherry and Nut Crisps

These small flap jack-type biscuits keep very well and have an excellent flavour.

Making time about 10 minutes
Baking time about 15 minutes

4 oz (100 g) demerara sugar
4 oz (100 g) spread for baking
4 oz (100 g) golden syrup
4 oz (100 g) plain flour
3 oz (75 g) rolled oats
1 oz (25 g) ground almonds
1½ oz (40g) flaked chopped almonds
2 oz (50 g) glacé cherries, chopped

Heat the oven to 180°c/160Fan/Gas 4 and grease several baking sheets.

Put the sugar, spread and syrup in a saucepan and heat gently until the sugar has dissolved.

Add all the remaining ingredients to the pan and mix very thoroughly and then leave to cool.

Roll the mixture into small balls each about the size of a walnut and place on the baking sheets, allowing room for them to spread slightly.

Bake for 15 minutes until they are a pale golden brown. Leave to harden for 1 minute and then lift off and leave to cool on a wire rack. Store in an airtight tin.

Makes about 36 cherry and nut crisps

Brandy Snaps

The quantities given in this recipe result in a lot of brandy snaps but they keep very well in an airtight tin. If only a few are required it is easy to make half the quantity. The mixture does not take long to make but it does take a little time to lift the brandy snaps from the baking sheet and roll them up.

Making time about 8 minutes
Baking time about 8 minutes

4 oz (100 g) butter
4 oz (100 g) demerara sugar
4 oz (100 g) golden syrup
4 oz (100 g) plain flour
1 level teaspoon ground ginger
1 teaspoon lemon juice

Heat the oven to 160°c/140Fan/Gas 3. Thoroughly grease several baking sheets and oil the handles of four wooden spoons.

Put the butter, sugar and syrup in a saucepan and heat gently until the butter and sugar have dissolved. Allow the mixture to cool slightly and then sift in the flour and ginger. Stir well, adding the lemon juice. Put the mixture on the baking sheet in teaspoonfuls at least 4 inches (10 cm) apart. It is best only to put four spoonfuls on the baking sheets at a time.

Cook in the oven for about 8 minutes until the snaps are a golden brown. Remove from the oven and leave for a few minutes to firm, then lift from the tin with a sharp knife, using a sawing movement. At once, roll around the handle of the wooden spoons and leave to set on a wire rack. Then slip out the spoons.

Store in an airtight tin as soon as they are cold.

They may be served just as they are with ice cream, mousses or soufflés but they are also good if you fill them with a little whipped cream and serve them with fruit.

Makes 30 brandy snaps

Chocolate Biscuits

These biscuits are fun to make as they can be marked and deco-rated as the fancy takes you. Flatten the biscuits, using either a fork, knife or potato masher, to give them an attractive finish.

Making time about 10 minutes
Baking time about 10 minutes

8 oz (225 g) spread for baking
4 oz (100 g) caster sugar
1 teaspoon vanilla extract
8 oz (225 g) self-raising flour
2 oz (50 g) drinking chocolate

Heat the oven to 190°c/170Fan/Gas 5 and grease two or three large baking sheets.

Cream the spread and sugar together with the vanilla essence until soft and then work in the flour and chocolate.

Divide the dough into small pieces each about the size of a walnut and place them, well spaced, on a baking sheet. Then flatten each biscuit with either a fork, round-bladed knife or a potato masher to make an attractive pattern on top.

Bake in the oven for about 8 to 10 minutes. Be careful not to let the biscuits brown too much as this will cause them to be bitter.

Leave the biscuits to harden for 1 minute on a baking sheet and then lift them off and leave to cool on a wire rack.

If liked, sprinkle the biscuits with a little sieved icing sugar when they come out of the oven.

Makes about 36 biscuits

Chocolate Cream Fingers

These are very similar to a well-known biscuit that is bought in shops; my family think these are far nicer and are always asking me to make them. Rolling the dough out on greaseproof paper makes it easy to handle.

Making time about 20 minutes
Baking time about 15 to 20 minutes

Biscuits
4 oz (100 g) plain flour
½ level teaspoon baking powder
2 level tablespoons cocoa
2 oz (50 g) spread for baking
2 oz (50 g) caster sugar
1 level tablespoon golden syrup

Filling
1 oz (25 g) spread for baking
2 oz (50 g) icing sugar
2 level teaspoons cocoa
a few drops vanilla extract

Heat the oven to 160°c/140Fan/Gas 3. Grease two baking sheets.

Place all the biscuit ingredients together in a bowl and work together until they are blended. Then turn the mixture onto a lightly sugared table and knead until smooth.

Roll out the dough to about ¼ inch (5 mm) thickness on a sheet of sugared greaseproof paper and then cut into fingers about 1 inch (2.5 cm) wide and about 2½ inches (6.25 cm) long. Carefully lift each finger onto a baking sheet and prick each two or three times. Bake in the oven for 15 to 20 minutes, lift off and leave to cool on a wire rack.

For the filling, put all the ingredients in a bowl and beat well until smooth and creamy. Use to sandwich the biscuits together in pairs.

Makes about 12 chocolate cream fingers

Chocolate Almond Biscuits

This recipe is an ideal way of using up those slices of toast left over from breakfast and any broken biscuits at the bottom of the tin.

Making time about 20 minutes
Baking time about 15 to 20 minutes

4 oz (100 g) toasted bread
4 oz (100 g) broken plain biscuits
3 oz (75 g) plain flour
2 oz (50 g) caster sugar
2 oz (50 g) drinking chocolate
2 oz (50 g) ground almonds
6 oz (175 g) spread for baking

Heat the oven to 160°c/140Fan/Gas 3 and grease several baking sheets.

Trim any crusts from the toast and then break it into pieces and put, with the biscuits, in a blender and run for a few seconds until they are reduced to fine breadcrumbs. Turn these into a large bowl.

Add the flour, sugar, chocolate and almonds to the crumbs and mix lightly. Add the spread and rub in with the fingertips and then gradually work the mixture together until you have a smooth firm dough.

Divide the mixture into small balls and put these on the baking sheet, pressing them flat with two fingers. Bake in the oven for about 15 to 20 minutes until they are firm.

Leave to cool for a few minutes on the baking sheet and then lift off and leave to cool on a wire rack.

Makes about 36 crunchy biscuits

Toll House Cookies

These biscuits are very easy to make and the children love finding the pieces of chocolate in them.

Making time about 15 minutes
Baking time about 10 to 12 minutes

4 oz (100 g) spread for baking
2 oz (50 g) light soft brown sugar
1 egg
1 teaspoon vanilla extract
8 oz (225 g) plain flour
½ level teaspoon bicarbonate of soda
2 to 3 oz (50 to 75 g) chocolate chips

Heat the oven to 190°c/170Fan/Gas 5. Grease two or three baking sheets.

Put the spread in a bowl with the sugar and beat well until soft and creamy and then work in all the remaining ingredients until the mixture forms a stiff dough.

Divide the mixture into small pieces. Put these on the baking sheets and then press them flat with the palm of your hand.

Bake the cookies in the oven for 10 to 12 minutes until they are a pale golden brown. Lift them off and leave to cool on a wire rack.

Makes about 28 to 30 cookies

Crisp Dutch Cookies

It is worthwhile using butter for this recipe as the flavour does come through.

Making time about 15 minutes
Baking time about 15 to 20 minutes

½ oz (12½ g) custard powder
6 oz (175 g) plain flour
5 oz (150 g) soft butter
3 oz (75 g) caster sugar
1 egg yolk

Sift together the custard powder and flour.

Cream the butter and sugar until the mixture is really soft and fluffy and then beat in the egg yolk. Mix in the flour until the mixture is well blended and smooth.

Put the mixture into a piping bag fitted with a large rose nozzle and pipe it onto a greased baking sheet in 3 zig-zag patterns about 1¾ inches (4.5 cm) wide and 10 inches (25 cm) long. Chill in the refrigerator for 30 minutes.

Heat the oven to 180°c/160Fan/Gas 4 and bake the cookies for 15 to 20 minutes or until they are pale golden brown at the edges. Remove from the oven and, while they are still warm, cut each zig-zag into 6 pieces. Leave to cool on a wire rack.

Makes 18 cookies

Honey Nut Cookies

A different type of cookie that is perfect for coffee mornings or bring-and-buy stalls.

Making time about 10 minutes
Baking time about 12 to 15 minutes

1 oz (25 g) plain chocolate
1 oz (25 g) spread for baking
1 level tablespoon thick honey
1 egg, beaten
2 oz (50 g) caster sugar
3 oz (75 g) plain flour
2 oz (50 g) walnuts, finely chopped

Heat the oven to 180°c/160Fan/Gas 4 and grease three baking sheets.

Break the chocolate into small pieces and place in a basin, together with the spread and honey, and stand it over a pan of simmering water until the chocolate and spread have melted. Remove from the heat and leave to cool slightly. Stir in the remaining ingredients.

Drop the mixture in small spoonfuls onto the baking sheets, leaving room for spreading.

Bake for 12 to 15 minutes until the cookies have risen slightly and are firm. Leave to cool for 1 minute, then lift off and leave on a wire rack to cool completely. Store in an airtight tin.

Makes 20 cookies

Orange Butter Cookies

It is well worth using butter for these cookies as the flavour really does come through. They are rather good if served with strawberries and cream.

Making time about 10 minutes
Baking time 10 to 15 minutes

4 oz (100 g) soft butter
4 oz (100 g) caster sugar
1 egg yolk
1 tablespoon orange juice
grated rind of 1 small orange
6 oz (175 g) plain flour
1 level teaspoon baking powder

Put the butter in a bowl with the sugar and beat together until light and creamy and then add the egg yolk, orange juice and rind and mix very well.

Add the flour and baking powder and work into the mixture until a dough is formed. Knead lightly until the mixture will leave the bowl quite clean.

Leave in a cool place for about 1 hour.

Heat the oven to 200°c/180Fan/Gas 4.

Divide the mixture into small balls, place these on the baking sheets and flatten them with a damp fork. Bake in the oven for 10 to 15 minutes until they are a pale golden brown all over. Lift from the baking sheets and leave to cool on a wire rack.

Makes 24 orange butter cookies

Peanut Butter Cookies

Most children love peanut butter and it is always in the store cupboard.

Making time about 10 minutes
Baking time about 12 to 15 minutes

8 oz (225 g) self-raising flour
3 oz (75 g) spread for baking
2 oz (50 g) crunchy peanut butter
2 level tablespoons thin honey
1 level tablespoon light soft brown sugar

Heat the oven to 180°c/160Fan/Gas 4 and grease two large baking sheets.

Put the flour in a bowl and add the spread, cut into small pieces, together with the peanut butter and rub in with your fingertips until the mixture resembles fine breadcrumbs.

Put the honey and sugar in a small pan and warm together until the sugar has dissolved. Then pour into the flour and mix very well with a fork to form a firm dough.

Turn onto a lightly floured table and knead lightly. Divide the mixture into 20 pieces, roll into balls and place, well spaced, on the baking sheets. Then press the balls flat with a damp fork.

Bake for about 12 to 15 minutes until they are a pale golden brown. Leave them on the baking sheet to harden for a few minutes and then lift them off and leave to cool on a wire rack until quite cold. Store in an airtight tin.

Makes about 20 cookies

Raisin Walnut Cookies

The raisins and walnuts in these cookies combine well to give a very good flavour.

Making time about 15 minutes
Baking time about 10 to 12 minutes

4 oz (100 g) spread for baking
4 oz (100 g) light soft brown sugar
1 egg, beaten
1 teaspoon vanilla extract
½ level teaspoon bicarbonate of soda
8 oz (225 g) plain flour
4 oz (100 g) raisins
2 oz (50 g) walnuts, chopped

Heat the oven to 190°c/170Fan/Gas 5. Grease two or three baking sheets.

Put the spread in a bowl with the sugar and beat well until soft and creamy and then work in all the remaining ingredients until the mixture forms a stiff dough.

Divide the mixture into small pieces. Place them on the baking sheets and then press them flat with the palm of the hand.

Bake in the oven for 10 to 12 minutes until the cookies are a pale golden brown and then lift them off and leave to cool on a wire rack. Store in an airtight tin.

Makes about 36 cookies

Coconut Crunchjacks

These are similar to flap jacks but the addition of coconut gives a crisp texture that is always popular.

Making time about 10 minutes
Baking time about 40 to 45 minutes

5 oz (150 g) spread for baking
5 oz (150 g) demerara sugar
5 oz (150 g) rolled oats
1 oz (25 g) desiccated coconut

Heat the oven to 160°c/140Fan/Gas 3 and grease a shallow baking tin about 11 × 7 inches (27.5 × 17.5 cm).

Cream the spread and sugar together and then add the oats and coconut and work the mixture together.

Press this into the tin and bake in the oven for about 40 to 45 minutes until it is golden brown

Remove from the oven and leave to cool in the tin for about 10 minutes. Then mark into 18 squares or fingers and leave in the tin until quite cold.

Lift out and store in an airtight container.

Makes 18 coconut crunchjacks

Melting Moments

These are simple to make and all the ingredients are likely to be found in the store cupboard. They are very popular in our house, so I usually make up double the quantity.

Making time about 10 minutes
Baking time about 20 minutes

3 oz (75 g) spread for baking
3 oz (75 g) caster sugar
half a beaten egg
a few drops of vanilla extract
1 oz (25 g) rolled oats
4 oz (100 g) self raising flour
a few rolled oats to coat
5 glacé cherries, quartered

Heat the oven to 160°c/140Fan/Gas 3. Grease two baking sheets.

Put the spread in a bowl with the sugar and beat together until soft and creamy. Work in the egg and vanilla extract. Add the oats and flour and work into the creamed mixture to make a dough.

Divide the mixture into 20 pieces and, with damp hands, roll these into balls. Toss each ball in rolled oats and then place about 2 inches (5 cm) apart on the baking sheets. Flatten each biscuit and place a quartered cherry in the centre of each. Bake in the oven for about 20 minutes until the biscuits are pale golden brown.

Lift them off and leave to cool on a wire rack.

Makes 20 melting moments

Melting Oat Crunchies

Children enjoy helping to make these crispy, wafer-thin biscuits. It takes no time to make the mixture, but it does take a while to roll it out.

Making time about 15 to 20 minutes
Baking time about 10 minutes

5 oz (150 g) butter
2 level tablespoons golden syrup
3 oz (75 g) plain flour
6 oz (175 g) caster sugar
3 oz (75 g) desiccated coconut
4 oz (100 g) rolled oats
1 oz (25 g) chopped walnuts

Heat the oven to 180°c/160Fan/Gas 4. Grease plenty of baking sheets.

Melt the butter and golden syrup in a pan over a low heat.

Put all the other ingredients in a bowl and bind together with the syrup mixture to form a fairly dry dough. It may be necessary to bring the dough together by kneading it lightly with the hand.

Roll the mixture into small balls the size of a walnut and place on the baking sheets, well spread out. Flatten them slightly with the palm of the hand. Bake them in the oven for about 10 minutes, until they are lightly browned at the edges.

Leave on the tray until slightly cool before removing onto a wire rack.

Makes about 40 biscuits

Ginger Fairings

A crisp biscuit with a mild ginger flavour.

Making time about 10 minutes
Baking time about 15 minutes

6 oz (175 g) self-raising flour
1 level teaspoon ground ginger
pinch of bicarbonate of soda
3 oz (75 g) caster sugar
3 oz (75 g) spread for baking
1 level tablespoon golden syrup

Heat the oven to 180°c/160Fan/Gas 4 and lightly grease three baking sheets.

Sift together into a bowl the flour, ginger and soda.

Put the sugar, spread and syrup in a saucepan and heat gently until the spread has melted. Then stir the mixture into the dry ingredients and mix to a stiff dough.

Shape into 24 small balls or place in teaspoonfuls on the baking sheets and bake for about 15 minutes until golden brown at the edges.

Leave to cool slightly and then lift off with a palette knife and leave to cool on a wire rack.

Makes 24 biscuits

Grantham Gingerbreads

Do not be surprised at the first bite – these biscuits are hollow in the centre.

Making time about 15 minutes
Baking time about 20 to 30 minutes

4 oz (100 g) spread for baking
12 oz (35S0 g) caster sugar
1 large egg, beaten
9 oz (250 g) self-raising flour
1 to 2 level teaspoons ground ginger

Heat the oven to 150°c/130Fan/Gas 2 and well grease about three baking sheets.

Cream the spread and sugar until soft and then beat in the egg. Sieve the flour with the ginger and add it to the mixture and work to a firm dough.

Turn the dough onto a lightly floured table. Knead and then roll it into small balls, each about the size of a walnut.

Place these, fairly well apart, on a baking sheet and then bake in the oven for 20 to 30 minutes until they are well puffed up and lightly browned.

Lift off and leave to cool on a wire rack.

Makes about 30 gingerbreads

Ginger Snaps

These ginger biscuits are inexpensive to make. They are also quick as there is no stamping out of rounds – just cut slices from the roll.

Making time about 8 minutes
Baking time about 15 minutes

8 oz (225 g) plain flour
½ to 1 level teaspoon ground ginger
¼ level teaspoon bicarbonate of soda
2½ oz (62 g) spread for baking
3 fl oz (90 ml) golden syrup

Heat the oven to 200°c/180Fan/Gas 4. Lightly grease some baking trays

Sift the flour, ginger and soda into a bowl and then rub in the spread until the mixture resembles breadcrumbs. Add the golden syrup and mix to a stiff dough – it is easier to use your hands for this stage. Roll the dough into a flat sausage and chill this for about 30 minutes in the refrigerator.

Cut the roll into thin slices and arrange on the baking tray. Bake the slices in the oven for about 15 minutes or until they are a pale ginger colour all over.

Remove the biscuits from the oven and leave them to cool on a wire rack.

Makes about 24 ginger snaps

Ginger Thins

If liked, make double the quantity of this mixture, keep half in the deep freeze and bake the remainder. When required, take the mixture from the freezer, leave it to thaw at room temperature and then bake as below.

Making time about 12 minutes
Baking time about 8 to 10 minutes

8 oz (225 g) plain flour
1½ level teaspoons ground ginger
4 oz (100 g) butter
6 oz (175 g) light soft brown sugar
1 small egg, beaten

Sieve the flour and ginger into a bowl, add the butter, cut into small pieces, and rub it in with your fingertips until the mixture resembles fine breadcrumbs.

Add the sugar and sufficient egg to bind the mixture to a firm dough.

Knead lightly and roll into a sausage about 2 inches (5 cm) in diameter. Wrap in cling film or foil and place in the refrigerator until really firm.

Heat the oven to 190°c/170Fan/Gas 5 and grease some baking sheets.

Cut the roll into thin slices. Place these, well spaced, on the baking sheets and bake for 8 to 10 minutes until they are pale golden brown at the edges.

Remove them from the oven, leave on the tray for 1 minute, then lift them onto the wire rack and leave to cool. Store in an airtight tin.

Makes about 24 ginger thins

Hazelnut Macaroons

These are cheaper to make than almond macaroons – and are very good in their own right.

Making time about 20 minutes
Baking time about 20 to 30 minutes

4 oz (100 g) hazelnuts
3 egg whites
8 oz (225 g) caster sugar
1 oz (25 g) ground rice

Heat the oven to 180°c/160Fan/Gas 4 and cover two or three baking sheets with silicone paper.

Place the hazelnuts in a dish and put them in the oven for a few minutes. Then tip them onto a clean tea towel, rub them well together and the skins will flake off. Place the nuts in the blender and grind to a fine powder. Tip this into a large bowl with 2 of the egg whites. Add the sugar and ground rice and beat well together for 3 to 4 minutes. Then gradually work in the extra egg white; it may not be necessary to add all the egg white if the mixture is very runny. Leave to stand for 5 minutes.

Place the mixture in small spoonfuls, well spaced, on the silicone paper and bake in the oven for 20 to 30 minutes until set and firm. If liked, the mixture may be put into a piping bag fitted with a ½ inch (1.25 cm) plain pipe and piped onto the paper.

Makes about 18 to 24 macaroons

Old English Jumbles

Jumbles are traditionally made in the shape of an 'S'. However, if time is short you will find it quicker to roll out small balls which take up less room on the baking sheet.

Making time about 10 minutes
Baking time about 15 to 20 minutes

2½ oz (62 g) caster sugar
2½ oz (62 g) butter or spread for baking
1 egg yolk
grated rind of 1 lemon
1 oz (25 g) ground almonds
5 oz (150 g) plain flour

Heat the oven to 180°c/160Fan/Gas 4 and lightly grease two baking sheets.

Cream the butter or spread with the sugar until light and fluffy, then beat in the egg yolk and the remaining ingredients. Take small pieces of the dough, roll each out into a strip and then form it into a letter 'S' and lay it on the baking sheet. Repeat with the remaining dough. Alternatively, divide the mixture into small balls, place on the baking sheet and press flat with two fingers.

Bake in the oven for about 15 to 20 minutes until the biscuits are tinged a pale golden brown at the edges.

Lift them off and leave to cool on a wire rack. These biscuits keep well if stored in an airtight tin.

Makes about 20 biscuits, depending on the shape

Easter Biscuits

Use butter for these biscuits as the flavour really does come through.

Making time about 15 minutes
Baking time about 12 to 15 minutes

6 oz (175 g) butter
4 oz (100 g) caster sugar
finely grated rind of 1 lemon
2 egg yolks
8 oz (225 g) plain flour
2 oz (50 g) currants
a little egg white and extra caster sugar to glaze

Heat the oven to 180°c/160Fan/Gas 4 and lightly grease two baking sheets.

Cream the butter with the sugar and lemon rind until light and fluffy, work in the egg yolks and then stir in the flour and currants and knead lightly until smooth. Leave the mixture in the refrigerator or a cool place for about 1 hour.

Roll out the dough on a lightly floured table to ⅛ inch (3 mm) thickness and cut into rounds with a fluted 3 inch (7.5 cm) cutter. Brush with a little lightly beaten egg white, dredge with caster sugar, lift onto a baking sheet and bake in the oven for 12 to 15 minutes or until just golden brown.

Lift onto a wire rack and leave to cool. Store in an airtight tin.

Makes about 24 biscuits

Index